Crowe, Chris
Up Close:Justice
Thurgood Marshall

# THURGOOD MARSHALL

**AVAILABLE UP CLOSE TITLES:**

**FUTURE UP CLOSE TITLES:**

# UP*close:*

# THURGOOD MARSHALL

*a twentieth-century life by*
***CHRIS CROWE***

VIKING

VIKING

Published by Penguin Group

Penguin Young Readers Group, 345 Hudson Street, New York, New York 10014, U.S.A.

Penguin Group (Canada), 90 Eglinton Avenue East, Suite 700, Toronto, Ontario,
Canada M4P 2Y3 (a division of Pearson Penguin Canada Inc.)

Penguin Books Ltd, 80 Strand, London WC2R 0RL, England

Penguin Ireland, 25 St Stephen's Green, Dublin 2, Ireland (a division of Penguin Books Ltd)

Penguin Group (Australia), 250 Camberwell Road, Camberwell, Victoria 3124, Australia
(a division of Pearson Australia Group Pty Ltd)

Penguin Books India Pvt Ltd, 11 Community Centre, Panchsheel Park, New Delhi – 110 017, India

Penguin Group (NZ), 67 Apollo Drive, Rosedale, North Shore 0632, New Zealand
(a division of Pearson New Zealand Ltd)

Penguin Books (South Africa) (Pty) Ltd, 24 Sturdee Avenue, Rosebank, Johannesburg 2196,
South Africa

Penguin Books Ltd, Registered Offices: 80 Strand, London WC2R 0RL, England

First published in 2008 by Viking, a division of Penguin Young Readers Group

10  9  8  7  6  5  4  3  2  1

Photo credits can be found on page 251.
Every effort has been made to credit copyright holders.

LIBRARY OF CONGRESS CATALOGING-IN-PUBLICATION DATA

Crowe, Chris.
Up close : Thurgood Marshall / by Chris Crowe.
p. cm.
ISBN 978-0-670-06228-7 (hardcover)
1. Marshall, Thurgood, 1908–1993–Juvenile literature. 2. United States. Supreme Court–Biography–
Juvenile literature. 3. African American lawyers–Biography–Juvenile literature. 4. African American
judges–Biography–Juvenile literature.  I. Title.
KF8745.M34C76 2008
347.73'2634–dc22
[B]
2007042794

Printed in the U.S.A.      Set in Goudy      Book design by Jim Hoover

87222

For Crismon Lewis and Phyllis Fogelman,
two editors who took a chance on me.

# THURGOOD MARSHALL

# CONTENTS

*The interesting things that can go in a book, you can't write.*

—THURGOOD MARSHALL

# FOREWORD

**LIKE MOST KIDS** in my junior high school in 1967, I knew practically nothing about African Americans. Sure, I'd heard of Martin Luther King Jr. and his fight for equal rights, but as a white seventh-grader in a white California suburb, that fight seemed to have very little to do with me. The only African Americans I knew anything about were the famous professional athletes of my day: Willie Mays, Jim Brown, Muhammad Ali, Wilt Chamberlain, and Arthur Ashe. To my sports-addled brain, these men were the most important African Americans in the nation.

So in June 1967, when President Lyndon B. Johnson made the sudden—and to some, startling—announcement that he had nominated Thurgood Marshall to a seat on the U.S. Supreme Court, the news didn't make a ripple in my narrow little world. I didn't know who Thurgood Marshall was, didn't know what the Supreme Court did, and had no idea why the fact that Marshall was black made the president's nomination such a big deal.

At the time, it was all over my head, out of my reach, beyond my understanding.

So why would I want to write a book about Thurgood Marshall?

The short answer is Emmett Till.

In August 1955, Emmett, a fourteen-year-old African American from Chicago, was visiting family in the tiny Delta town of Money, Mississippi. While there, he unknowingly crossed a Jim Crow boundary and, as local sources put it, "got himself killed" by a group of white men.

For years I've been fascinated by Till's story, a frequently overlooked catalyst in the modern Civil Rights Movement, and as I studied and wrote about the case, I learned something that all historians know: nothing happens in a vacuum. Many events and many people helped set the stage for the murder of Emmett Till and for the impact his death would have on American society, but Thurgood Marshall figures more prominently than anyone or anything else. The murder and the trial generated headlines across the country, and the outrage at the inevitable acquittal of the killers helped spark the Montgomery Bus Boycott. From there, the rest is history.

Civil-rights history.

And that's a history with Thurgood Marshall's fingerprints all over it.

In 1954, the year I was born, Marshall was one of the most famous lawyers in the country; the African American press had dubbed him "Mr. Civil Rights" for his tireless legal efforts to challenge racial inequality. Unlike many civil-rights activists, Marshall believed that the law was the best—perhaps the only—way to overcome racism. Throughout his career, he used the law, his wits, and his exceptional courtroom skills to chip away at the wall that separated African Americans from mainstream society.

He may not be the best-known African American from the twentieth century—he's easily overshadowed by popular heroes like Jackie Robinson, Malcolm X, and Martin Luther King Jr.—but many people regard Thurgood Marshall as the most important African

American from that era. At the end of Marshall's career, journalist Juan Williams wrote, "If Whites could see Thurgood Marshall more clearly, they might see the most important Black man of this century—a man who rose higher than any Black person before him and who has had more effect on Black lives than any other person, Black or White."

Now you get to find out why.

# INTRODUCTION

## *David v. Goliath*

**ON MAY 17, 1954,** more than three hundred people jammed the main chamber of America's temple of law, the Supreme Court Building in Washington, D.C. Their whispers echoed in the cavernous marble courtroom as they waited for the nine Supreme Court justices to enter through the red velour drapes and take their seats behind the mahogany bench that faced the gallery. The court had a few minor items of business to take care of that day, but the bulk of the audience—nearly equal numbers of white and black Americans—was there to hear the decision on the case that had been named *Brown et al. v. Board of Education of Topeka.*

Thurgood Marshall and his team of lawyers and

*Thurgood Marshall in front of the Supreme Court Building during his days as a lawyer for the NAACP.*

consultants from the National Association for the Advancement of Colored People (NAACP) sat in the packed chamber, shackled by the overwhelming pressure riding on this announcement. They would soon learn if they had won or lost their attack on the Goliath of racism, the Jim Crow attitudes and traditions that claimed that segregation—separation of the races—was not only legal but also *beneficial* to African American schoolchildren. Lawyers on both sides of the case knew that Jim Crow laws had begun when racist white Southerners, angry at the new freedoms President Lincoln and the Civil War had earned for African Americans, created laws that barred former slaves and their families from basic constitutional freedoms such as the right to vote. Segregation policy also banned African Americans from mixing with whites in public places like restaurants, theaters, and schools. Both sides knew that these Jim Crow laws, defended more than once by the U.S. Supreme Court, had stood firm for nearly a century.

Marshall's team realized that their chances for victory were slimmer than a cotton thread. John W. Davis, one of the greatest lawyers of his time, led the opposition and was backed by racists and segregationists from the South with a century of legal precedent, three hundred years of racist tradition, and overwhelming political and financial support on their side. To add to the segregationists' advantage, their legal arguments were made to an all-white panel of Supreme Court judges.

The NAACP team, on the other hand, was an underfunded group of young lawyers battling to overturn Supreme Court precedent and centuries of racial oppression, discrimination, and segregation.

The long march to this court had been exhilarating and frustrating. For four years, Marshall and his NAACP colleagues had worked on this case day and night, battled racist lawyers and judges, and endured one legal defeat after another. The grueling battle had been an emotional and physical drain on Marshall, the NAACP's lead attorney in the case. His wife, Buster, had been seriously ill for weeks leading up to the *Brown* announcement, and with his time-consuming travel commitments and legal preparations, he had little time to spend with her. His prolonged absences from home and her poor health strained their marriage, but despite the stress, Mrs. Marshall made it to Washington on May 17 to support her husband.

Marshall was lucky to be there himself. On May 16 he had been in Mobile, Alabama, on NAACP business and was preparing to travel to Los Angeles when he received a tip that the Court planned to announce a decision on *Brown* the next day. He immediately canceled his Los Angeles trip and flew back to Washington.

On this Monday in May, Supreme Court business began at noon, as it usually did. The nine justices, dressed in their black silk robes, entered and took their seats at the head of the courtroom. Marshall tried to read their faces for a sign of how they had voted, but the justices gave no clue regarding their decision.

The court was called to order, and the justices turned their attention to the first item of business: granting 118 lawyers admission to the Supreme Court bar. With that over, Justice Tom C. Clark and Justice William O. Douglas read short decisions on two cases.

At 12:52 Chief Justice Earl Warren picked up a sheaf of papers and said, "I have for announcement the judgment and opinion of the Court in *Oliver Brown v.*

*Board of Education of Topeka*." The audience fell silent as they focused on the chief justice for an announcement of victory or defeat.

In a powerful, clear voice, the silver-haired chief justice began reading: "These cases come to us from the States of Kansas, South Carolina, Virginia, and Delaware. They are premised on different facts and different local conditions, but a common legal question justifies their consideration together in this consolidated opinion." Anticipation charged the room with tension, but the audience remained silent, carefully listening to the chief justice's detailed explanation of the case's background.

The waiting tortured Marshall. After several minutes, he couldn't tell where the chief justice was headed with his opinion, and the uncertainty seemed unbearable. He and his fellow lawyers had poured their souls into this case, and defeat would be crushing not only to them but also to all African Americans who longed for the equal rights they had been promised by the U.S. Constitution. Anxious as they were for answers, everyone in the courtroom had no choice but to be patient as the judge plowed through the opinion.

"In approaching this problem," he read, "we cannot turn the clock back to 1868, when the Amendment was adopted, or even to 1896, when *Plessy v. Ferguson* was written. We must consider public education in the light of its full development and its present place in American life."

Marshall knew this legal background as well as anyone, but what he and everyone else present ached to hear was the answer to a simple question:

Would Jim Crow be upheld or struck down?

# ONE

## *Black and White: A Nation Divided*

**WHERE DOES** the story of Thurgood Marshall begin? Born in 1908, he eventually became one of America's most important lawyers and civil-rights warriors, and he capped his illustrious career by serving as the first African American on the United States Supreme Court.

But his story, or at least the story of the society that he helped transform, begins much earlier than that.

It begins with a colony of English immigrants who, for reasons difficult to comprehend today, decided to import slaves from Africa. The struggle to survive in this rugged New World exacted a heavy price from the earliest settlers, and the lure of cheap slave labor may have been too powerful to ignore. Of course, the institution of slavery had been established in Europe centuries before the American colonists entered the trade, so perhaps some people rationalized slavery by citing historical precedent. Others may have cited mis-interpretations from the Bible, and still others might have justified slavery as a sheer economic necessity.

Whatever the case, by 1670, when the African slave trade had been established in several colonies, many citizens accepted the business, and slavery grad-ually became commonplace in America—so com-monplace, in fact, that when the Founding Fathers penned the Declaration of Independence that boldly proclaimed, "We hold these truths to be self-evident, that all men are created equal," they knew that the democratic principles of the Declaration, and later of the U.S. Constitution, would not apply to slaves.

Slavery flourished in America for nearly 250 years, and even after the Emancipation Proclamation in 1863 and the Thirteenth, Fourteenth, and Fifteenth Amendments were passed after the Civil War to free slaves and guarantee them basic rights, U.S. law con-tinued to limit the freedoms of African Americans for another century. During that time, like all people of color in America, Marshall's ancestors suffered physically, emotionally, and economically because of the nation's unwillingness to extend constitutional protection to every citizen.

And, like his ancestors, Thurgood Marshall grew up in a country determined to discriminate against its nonwhite citizens, and America—as he learned from school and from personal experience—had always been pretty good at finding ways to keep black people "in their place."

From the time our nation was founded, many white Americans believed that people with dark skin were a subhuman species and therefore weren't entitled to—or even capable of enjoying—the same rights and privileges as whites. For example, in 1705 Virginia legislators passed a law "declaring the Negro, Mulatto, and Indian slaves within this dominion, to be real estate." As property, slaves had no legal rights and no legal identity, and that meant they could be bought and sold, abused and mistreated, even murdered by their owners.

Racist laws like these created a culture that encouraged slavery and racial discrimination in America while it grew from thirteen colonies into an independent nation. As new states were formed, most established their own laws regarding slaves and free African Americans. States like Massachusetts and Vermont tried to guarantee the rights of all citizens, regardless of race, but states that depended on slavery did whatever they could to maintain white dominance.

Unfortunately, the federal government defended states' rights to discriminate against African Americans. In 1856, only a few years after Thurgood Marshall's grandfather was born into slavery, the U.S. Supreme Court heard the case of *Scott v. Sandford*. Dred Scott, a slave who had lived with his owner in the free states of Illinois and Wisconsin, demanded to be set free when his owner died in 1843. His demands were ignored, and in 1846 Scott sued for his freedom. After a decade of legal defeats and appeals, the case landed in the U.S. Supreme Court. In 1857 the Court ruled against Dred Scott by declaring that African Americans, slave or free, had no constitutional rights. Chief justice Roger Brooke Taney said that the framers of the Constitution had believed that people of African descent were "beings of an inferior order, and altogether unfit to associate with the white race, either in social or political relations; and so far inferior, that they had no rights which the white man was bound to respect; and that the negro might justly and lawfully be reduced to slavery for his benefit."

The justice went on to answer the question at the heart of the case: Does the Constitution—and the United States government—regard African Americans as citizens? Chief Justice Taney concluded, "We think they are not, and that they are not included, and were not intended to be included, under the word 'citizens' in the Constitution, and can therefore claim none of the rights and privileges which that instrument provides for and secures to citizens of the United States."

Despite the strenuous objections of abolitionists, the Dred Scott decision reinforced slavery and racism, and it shattered the hopes of African Americans who had longed for legal protection.

As the United States approached its one hundredth birthday, however, some of its leaders believed that the rights established in the nation's founding documents ought to be extended to all male Americans. Slaves and abolitionists celebrated President

Abraham Lincoln's 1863 proclamation, and the Union's victory in the Civil War in 1865 promised to change the cruel racist tradition that had deep roots in the Southern states. Soon after the Civil War, Congress drafted a constitutional amendment designed to limit the political activities of former Rebels but more importantly to grant the rights of citizenship and constitutional protection to "all persons born or naturalized in the United States" and to guarantee all American citizens "the equal protection of the laws." In 1868 that amendment, now known as the Fourteenth Amendment, was approved by a majority of states and passed into law.

The Founding Fathers had created the Constitution as a flexible set of laws that would protect the basic rights of U.S. citizens. Knowing that no legal document was perfect, the authors of the Constitution stipulated that its laws could be interpreted by the Supreme Court or amended by Congress in order to meet the nation's changing needs. Congress intended the Fourteenth Amendment, and the Fifteenth Amendment in 1870, to overturn the Dred Scott decision and give former slaves rights that had previously been enjoyed only by white male Americans, including the rights to vote, to own property, and to gain an education.

Unfortunately, the positive effects of the Fourteenth Amendment were short-lived. By the late 1870s Southern states ignored parts of the Constitution they didn't agree with and established racist policies—eventually called Jim Crow laws—that stripped African Americans of their newly gained civil rights.

The term *Jim Crow* soon became widely used in the South. It had originated in the 1830s, not in politics but in a minstrel show where a white performer blackened his face and sang and danced as a foolish old "Negro." By the 1850s the Jim Crow character became a regular feature in minstrel shows, reinforcing the negative stereotype of African Americans among white people. Jim Crow was later associated—though no one knows exactly how—with the wide-ranging local and state laws and attitudes that deprived black people of the freedoms enjoyed by whites. Eventually the Jim Crow stranglehold gave white society total control of elections, schools, and police, leaving African Americans with no way to protect themselves or to fight for change.

By the end of the nineteenth century, the contagion of racial segregation had spread throughout the United States, and once again the Supreme Court, instead of protecting the rights of African Americans, issued a decision that undercut their freedoms.

The case began in 1892 when Homer Plessy, a man who was only one-eighth African American, purchased a first-class ticket on the East Louisiana Railroad in order to challenge a new state law that mandated separate seating for blacks and whites. When Plessy took his first-class seat, in the white section, the conductor ordered him into the black car. Plessy refused to move, was thrown off the train, arrested, and convicted for violating the state segregation law.

When discussing the famous case years later, Marshall pointed out the absurdity of the law:

> Because one of your great-grandparents was a Negro, you are told that you must sit in a special coach on the train, and you haven't the right to complain—and certainly not the right to bring the company to trial. I'll bet nobody had to take a white man by the arm and tell him what coach *he* could sit in.

*The justices of the U.S. Supreme Court that issued the* Plessy v. Ferguson *decision in 1896.*

Plessy should have sent one-eighth of himself with the conductor and left seven-eighths of himself in the white coach.

Plessy appealed the conviction, and his case eventually reached the U.S. Supreme Court at the end of 1895. Many Americans hoped the Court would rule in favor of Plessy and grant African Americans the same rights as white Americans, but the justices on the Court had no sympathy for Plessy, and in 1896 they voted seven to one (Justice David Josiah Brewer did not participate in this case) against his appeal.

"We think the enforced separation of the races," wrote Justice Henry B. Brown, "neither abridges the privileges or immunities of the colored man, . . . nor denies him the equal protection of the laws, within the meaning of the fourteenth amendment." Speaking for the majority of the Court, he went on to say that state separate-but-equal laws were legal according to the Court's interpretation of the U.S. Constitution.

Justice Brown's concluding statement dealt a devastating blow to African Americans who had hoped they could use the Fourteenth Amendment's promise of "equal protection of the laws" to argue that they deserved the same privileges and protections that white people had. Perhaps to convince African Americans that they would never have true equality in the United States or just to warn civil-rights activists and other rabble-rousers against using legal challenges to fight for equal rights, Justice Brown wrote that "legislation is powerless to eradicate racial instincts, or to abolish distinctions based upon physical differences, and the attempt to do so can only result in accentuating the difficulties of the present situation."

For African Americans, the dream of civil rights had just turned into a nightmare.

In that darkest of nightmares, especially in the years immediately after the *Plessy* case, many people overlooked a crack in the Supreme Court's ruling, a dissenting opinion that in the hands of the right lawyer might someday provide the means to overturn segregation.

That crack lay buried in the minority opinion written by Justice John Marshall Harlan, the lone dissenter in the seven-to-one vote in the *Plessy* decision. As a gift to some future civil-rights lawyer, Justice Harlan left a reminder in the Court record that the United States government and its laws must protect all citizens. "The destinies of the two races in this country," Harlan wrote, "are indissolubly linked together, and the interests of both require that the common government of all shall not permit the seeds of race hate to be planted under the sanction of law." Unfortunately, Justice Harlan's opinion had no effect on his fellow justices, and *Plessy v. Ferguson* established a legal precedent that sentenced African Americans to sixty more years of suffocating racial discrimination and segregation.

In 1908 Thurgood Marshall was born into a Jim Crow society that traced its roots—and its legal precedents—back to racist state laws supported by Supreme Court cases such as *Scott v. Sandford* and *Plessy v. Ferguson*. This society would heap barriers, prejudice, and hatred upon him solely because of the color of his skin. This society would do whatever it could to keep him and all other African Americans poor, uneducated, and uninvolved.

In less than fifty years, however, this society would be turned upside down when Thurgood Marshall argued the most monumental civil-rights case in American history.

# TWO

## *A Baby Born into Jim Crow*

**JULY 2, 1908.** Born to Willie and Norma Marshall in their apartment at 543 McMechen Street, in Baltimore, their second child, a son named Thoroughgood (later changed to Thurgood) Marshall.

His unusual first name came from his grandfather who had been born a slave. That grandfather had two first names, Thorney Good and Thoroughgood, the younger Marshall once told a reporter, "and he collected money on both of them. . . . He was in one of the those wars after the Civil War—the Cuba business with Teddy Roosevelt, I think. So he was entitled to some veterans' benefit checks, and my grandmother collected checks under both names until she died. Two checks for the same man."

What was America like when Marshall was born?

The hero of the Spanish-American War, Theodore Roosevelt, was serving his final months as president of the United States. About 89 million people lived in the nation's forty-six states, and approximately 10 percent of them were African American. Marshall's home state of Maryland had much greater racial diversity, with nearly 20 percent of its population made up of African American residents who, in nearly all cases, were oppressed by Jim Crow laws.

The America of 1908 was strikingly different from the country we know today. For example, less than half the population enjoyed the legal freedoms and protections that modern Americans take for granted. African Americans, of course, had precious few freedoms, but they weren't the only citizens who had been deprived of equal protection under the law. When Marshall was born, it was illegal for women to vote in national elections, but it was legal for children as young as seven or eight years old to work in backbreaking, dangerous jobs, sometimes for as little as ten cents a day.

Though Norma and Willie and Marshall's grandparents were thrilled at the arrival of this baby boy, none of them could have dreamed that one day he would become one of the most important legal figures in American history. Their inability to dream that big for Thoroughgood had nothing to do with a lack of ambition. Norma's mother, Mary Williams, had been a teacher at a private black academy in Baltimore, and Norma's sister Avonia was one of the first black teachers to land a job in a black public school. The family had always valued education, and even after Norma's father died, they sacrificed financially to keep her in college. In a time when few women attended college, even fewer black women did so, and it was expected that when a woman—black or white—married, she would drop out of college to devote herself to house-wifely duties.

Things were different for Norma. When she announced her plans to marry Willie Marshall, her mother convinced Willie not only that Norma should finish college but also that he should pay for it. Willie agreed, and a few weeks after their marriage in April 1905, Norma graduated from Coppin State College in Baltimore. Not long after her graduation, Norma and Willie's first child, William Aubrey Marshall, was born, and Norma put off her teaching career to stay home to tend Aubrey.

Willie Marshall came from a different background.

While in elementary school, he had been a trouble-making, wisecracking kid who had no fear of teachers or administrators, and his cocky attitude eventually ended his education. Willie never finished high school; years later Thurgood Marshall told a newspaper reporter why: "The high school notified my grandfather that my father had misbehaved. My grandfather went to the high school, took my father into the hall, and whipped him in the presence of all the other students. Pop was so embarrassed that he never went back to school." That humiliating experience ended Willie's formal education but not his relationship with his family. He continued to live at home and stayed busy with odd jobs. A few years later he started working in his family's grocery store in West Baltimore, where he learned not only the value of the dollar but also the importance of hard work.

In addition to learning the value of hard work, Willie Marshall also learned to be proud of his African heritage. With his light skin, it would have been easy for him to "pass"—that is, pass himself off as a white person—but Willie was not ashamed of his race. He understood that racial pride didn't have to mean racial intolerance, and even though he had suffered the indignities of racial segregation, he still had white friends. When he got older, he even had a good friend, a white Baltimore policeman named Captain Cook, who would sometimes visit the Marshalls' home. Racial tensions in Baltimore made many African Americans distrust the police force, but Willie Marshall preferred to judge people based on their behavior, not on the color of their skin. He once told his son, "There is no difference between a white snake and a black snake. They both bite." The younger Marshall would never forget his father's examples of pride and tolerance.

Before he met Norma, Willie Marshall left the family grocery store and began working as a porter for the Baltimore and Ohio Railroad, a steady job that would provide enough income to support him and a family. After their marriage Willie and Norma, comfortably situated in their hometown of Baltimore, set up house with high hopes for their children.

But even the most ambitious African American parents understood the reality of racial oppression, and the best they could hope for was that their children would one day attend black colleges and, with

lots of hard work and a little luck, might become professionals—doctors, dentists, or lawyers—who worked
exclusively in black neighborhoods.

When Marshall was born in 1908, American society still embraced Jim Crow segregation laws that
had been endorsed by the Supreme Court's 1896 *Plessy*
decision, and almost nowhere was the "separate but
equal" idea applied fairly. Most of the time, conditions
for blacks were separate but *un*equal, and there was
nothing that Thoroughgood Marshall's parents could
do about it.

Not that some people hadn't tried.

The tensions surrounding racial segregation and
discrimination fed an undercurrent of anger that
swirled just below the surface of American society.
African Americans were frustrated and angry because
of the second-class treatment they received in their
own country. Racist white Americans were frustrated
and angry because many blacks refused to accept
their place in segregated society. The racists hoped
blacks would follow the example of prominent African
American leader Booker T. Washington, who in 1895
had declared in a widely publicized speech, "No race

can prosper till it learns that there is as much dignity in tilling a field as in writing a poem. It is at the bottom of life that we must begin, not at the top."

Of course, everyone knew that Jim Crow traditions in the United States would guarantee that all African Americans would begin "at the bottom of life" and would remain there until the day they died.

This was the America into which Thoroughgood Marshall was born, and around the time of his birth, racial violence was all too common. According to NAACP records, from 1889 to 1918 more than 2,500 African Americans died at the hands of lynch mobs; at least fifteen of those lynchings took place in Marshall's home state of Maryland.

Like all African Americans, Marshall's family understood that the constant threat of violence usually had nothing to do with their behavior but everything to do with the color of their skin, and it was inevitable that fear of racial violence affected their attitudes and behavior. To avoid antagonizing racists, some blacks chose to follow Booker T. Washington's advice and do whatever they could to build productive lives within the confines of Jim Crow laws. Others found ways to combat racism by undermining segregation without drawing attention to themselves. It's not surprising, however, that some African Americans, wearied by centuries of abuse and second-class citizenship, erupted in anger. Race riots in Atlanta in 1906 and Springfield, Illinois, in 1908 showed that those eruptions always resulted in even worse conditions for blacks.

Just one year before Marshall's birth, one of America's most popular magazines, *The Saturday Evening Post*, published an article about a "solution" to the "race question" proposed by Mississippi governor James K. Vardaman. In the article Vardaman called on the government to take away African Americans' constitutional right to citizenship:

> The negro should never have been trusted with the ballot. He is different from the white man. He is congenitally unqualified to exercise the most responsible duty of citizenship. He is physically, mentally, morally, racially and eternally the white man's inferior. There is nothing in the history of his race, nothing in his individual character, nothing in his achieve-

ments of the past nor his promise for the future
which entitles him to stand side by side with
the white man at the ballot-box.

Vardaman's outrageous commentary was typical
racist ideology of the time. It also reflected the under-
lying racial attitudes that Thurgood Marshall would
battle for much of his legal career.

Fortunately, at the time of Marshall's birth, not
all whites believed the racist nonsense preached by
people like Vardaman, and, despite the constant threat
of violence, not all African Americans were prepared
to meekly accept a Jim Crow life. W. E. B. Du Bois and
more than thirty other African American activists met
in New York in 1905 to form the Niagara Movement,
an organization that rejected Booker T. Washington's
acceptance of Jim Crow life and instead insisted on a
more aggressive approach to counter American racism.
In language that foreshadowed the later Civil Rights
Movement, the Niagara organizers announced,

We claim for ourselves every single right that
belongs to a freeborn American, political, civil

*Four of the founders of the Niagara Movement, the organization that later merged with the NAACP. W. E. B. Du Bois is seated.*

and social; and until we get these rights we will never cease to protest and assail the ears of America. The battle we wage is not for ourselves alone but for all true Americans. It is a fight for ideals, lest this, our common fatherland, false to its founding, become in truth the land of the thief and the home of the slave—a byword and a hissing among the nations for its sounding pretensions and pitiful accomplishment.

Unfortunately, lack of financial and political support doomed Du Bois's Niagara Movement to failure. After struggling to keep the Niagara Movement alive for four years, Du Bois merged the organization with a group of white civil-rights activists to form the National Association for the Advancement of Colored People, the same civil-rights organization that twenty-five years later would employ a bright and ambitious young lawyer named Thurgood Marshall.

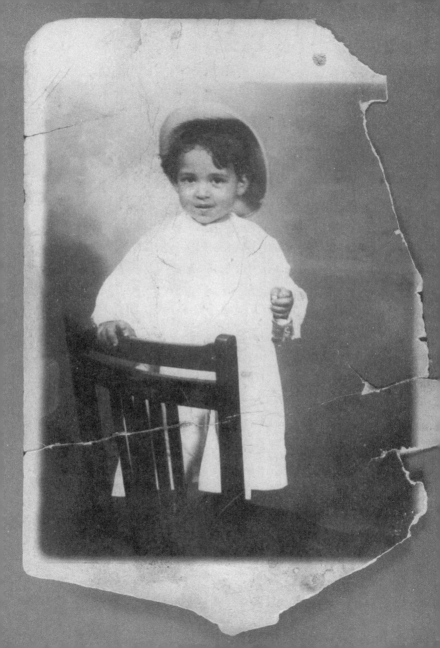

# THREE

## *Goody*

**THOROUGHGOOD MARSHALL** "was one of the most beautiful babies I have ever seen," recalled a family friend. For the first two years of his life, little Thoroughgood lived with his parents and older brother, Aubrey, in an apartment across the street from a Baltimore slaughterhouse. In 1910, when Aubrey was six and Thoroughgood was two, Norma's older sister Denmedia invited the Marshall family to move to New York City. The opportunity to live close to Norma's sister and the promise of a better job for Willie with the New York Central Railroad convinced the Marshalls to leave Baltimore and take up residence at 140th Street and Lenox Avenue in the Harlem neighborhood of New York City. Harlem

*Thurgood Marshall around the age of two.*

had already established itself as a thriving center for African American culture and business. Along a street near Harlem, however, stretched a banner that read, "This part of 135th Street guaranteed against Negro invasion," showing that racism in New York City was just as prominent as it had been in Baltimore.

A relative described Thoroughgood, nicknamed Goody, as a "timid little boy . . . a cry baby when he was small." Most of his crying had nothing to do with illness or weakness; it was an early sign of his shrewdness. When he was little, Goody was being treated for a hernia and overheard the doctor tell his mother, "See that he doesn't do any crying." Even as a child, Goody figured out how to exploit the doctor's orders, so whenever he didn't get his way, he cried. Unfortunately for him, his crying tactic didn't last for long. One of his aunts said that by the time Goody was five years old, "he stopped crying and became a pretty tough boy. Now, I don't know what caused the change. Maybe the boys slapped his head." Marshall remembered things differently. He recalled that he stopped being a crybaby when his mother finally caught on to his use of crying as manipulation, and to break him of it, bandaged his hernia tightly and "beat the stuffing out of him."

In 1914, when Goody was six years old, his grandmother broke her leg and the family had to return to Baltimore to help care for her. Back in the city of his birth, Goody started first grade at a two-story redbrick segregated elementary school on Division Street, a few blocks from his home. By this time he had grown tired of being teased about his nickname, so he talked his mother into changing his name on his birth certificate from Thoroughgood to Thurgood. "I didn't like having to spell 'Thoroughgood,'" he said. "It was too damned long, so I cut it. I didn't have nobody's permission, I just did it."

The feistiness and high energy that would one day characterize Marshall as a civil-rights lawyer made their first appearance in elementary school where, according to friend and journalist Carl Rowan, he spent a lot of time "goofing off, driving his mother crazy." One classmate recalled that Thurgood had to sit in the front of the room because he "was always playing, so they had to keep right on top of him." In addition to goofing off in class, he loved to tease. "He used to drive me crazy," said another childhood friend about the treatment she and her friend endured as his classmates.

Willie Marshall had learned the value of hard work when he was young, and he expected his boys to learn the same lesson. One of Thurgood's first jobs began when he was seven years old. He worked as a delivery boy in the afternoons for a local grocer named Mr. Hale. Marshall would gather items ordered by neighborhood customers, load them into his wagon, and deliver the goods to the customers' homes. He earned ten cents a day plus all he could eat, a job perk that was impossible for a young boy to pass up. On his second day of work, he gorged on candy and pickles and became so sick that Mr. Hale had to take him home. His boss later told Thurgood that he had added the all-you-can-eat perk to the job because he knew that Thurgood would be distracted by the candy and treats in the store, and if he allowed him to eat until he got sick, "you'd break yourself of the habit."

Thurgood wasn't a bad kid, and much of his elementary school mischief can be chalked up to boyish enthusiasm, but his rowdiness may also have been the result of his growing awareness of the racial tensions in his neighborhood and in the larger society around him. He sometimes overheard his parents discussing lynchings and other racist crimes, and even as a child raised within the safe confines of a close-knit family, he couldn't help but learn about—and face—some of the tragic consequences of Jim Crow society. In an interview in 1977, Marshall told a reporter:

> We used to have fights with the white kids, just on general principles. There was a white Catholic elementary school two blocks from Division Street, and for some reason, we didn't get along very well. They were practically all Italians, and we used to have periodic fights— not too bad. Maybe a rock here and there. It was fists, and eventually [the white school] let them out fifteen minutes before we got out, so that they could get home.

During Marshall's childhood, street skirmishes like this were all too common because of the terrible racial climate in Baltimore. Segregation laws in his hometown, Marshall said, were more rigid than in any other city in the country, and that limited his family's contact with whites. "The only relations [with white people] would be with the corner grocery store, nothing with people downtown, and that went through the whole time I was in Baltimore. . . . In the department stores downtown, a Negro was not allowed to buy anything off the counters, and if you went in the store, you were told to get the hell out."

As he grew up, Marshall learned that in addition to keeping the races separate, Jim Crow laws also humiliated blacks. He never forgot a particularly painful experience from his childhood. In some areas in downtown Baltimore, public restrooms weren't just segregated; they were reserved for whites only. "I remember very well that there were no toilet facilities available to Negroes in the downtown area," Marshall said, "and I remember one day, I had to go, and the only thing I could do was get on a trolley car and try to get home. And I did get almost in the house, when I ruined the front doorsteps. That gives you an idea what we went through."

Fighting white kids and living under the burden

of segregation turned the little boy everyone used to call Goody into a tough kid. "In Baltimore, where I was brought up, we lived on a respectable street, but behind us there were back alleys where the roughnecks and the tough kids hung out. . . . When it was time for dinner, my mother used to go to the front door and call my older brother. Then she'd go to the back door and call me."

Marshall's parents and extended family did their best to shield him from the harsh realities of racism, but his experiences in school and on the streets taught him about the dark side of life for minorities in America. When he was almost fifty, he could still vividly recall the first time he learned about the racial epithet that many people used to label him and his family: "I heard a kid call a Jewish boy I knew a kike to his face. I was about seven. I asked him why he didn't fight the kid. He asked me what I would do if somebody called me nigger—would I fight? That was a new one on me. I knew 'kike' was a dirty word but I hadn't known about 'nigger.' I went home and wanted to know right that minute what this all meant."

His parents explained the racist term to Thurgood,

but they made it clear then—and continued to do so throughout his youth—that regardless of what people called him, he was every bit as good, every bit as important as any other human being. "My dad and my mother both used to tell us that we had what everybody else had. And the fact that you happened to be a different color didn't mean anything. My dad would say that my mother was the prettiest brown-skinned woman in the world. And my mother would say, 'Brown-skinned? No, I'm the prettiest woman in the world.'"

Marshall loved his parents' strength, humor, and self-confidence, and their example forged in him an attitude that helped him endure the racist taunts and threats he would live with throughout his life.

When Marshall was eleven years old, a Washington, D.C., newspaper printed a sensational article about a white woman who claimed that two black men who had grabbed her umbrella and harassed her. Determined to teach the two alleged assailants—and all other blacks in the city—a lesson in Jim Crow respect, the woman's husband and his buddies decided they would lynch the two men. The mob of white vigilantes roamed the streets of Washington attacking any blacks they found. When Marshall heard about the mob violence, he worried that his light-skinned father would get caught in the wrong place at the wrong time. Angry blacks might mistake him for a white; angry whites might recognize him as a black. "He had a hell of a time," Marshall said. "The Negroes would run one place, the white folks were running the other. So he was running back and forth. Wherever he went, he was wrong."

Fortunately, not all of Marshall's education about race grew out of violence or the threat of it. When he was young, Norma often took him to her mother's home, and his grandmother doted on Marshall, teaching him to cook and giving him what seemed to her to be some very practical advice: "Your mother and father want you to be a dentist or a doctor, something like that. . . . And I hope you make it. But just in case you don't, I'm going to teach you how to cook. And you know why? You've never seen an unemployed black cook."

This woman had a powerful influence on Marshall. From her, he inherited his sense of humor, but he also admired her strength and determination. Over the years their conversations covered a wide range of topics, but Marshall especially remembered that she taught him about his black heritage and of the times immediately after the Civil War. "I would talk to her for hours on end, and her life went all the way back to the early days of the Negro, right after Reconstruction, and her husband knew all of the prominent Negroes in those days." Her stories eventually inspired him to study black history on his own, introducing him to some of the great activists and their philosophies. "From what she told me, I'd go and pull out books. The first one was Frederick Douglass."

Though Marshall's parents never had enough money to provide much in the way of luxuries, he said, "they provided something more precious—a lesson about the pervasiveness of racism, and that Negroes had to have some independence from white people. My father was very sensitive about the tiniest of nuances of racism," including the nuances of language. For example, instead of repeating the common saying "That's very white of you" to thank someone, Willie Marshall changed the racist expression to "That's very black of you." His mother taught her son to stand up against racism. "She didn't believe in physical fighting, but if you called her a 'negress' you'd have to fight her. Anyone she really hated she'd call a 'slitch.' Man or woman, anyone racially offensive was a 'slitch,' which was a cross between a slut and a bitch. I once told her, 'Mama, when you go for it, you really go for it.'" From her, Marshall learned to be strong, to work hard, and to be fearless in speaking his mind. "My mother—believe it or not, my father was the noisiest and loudest, but my mother was by far the strongest. My mother was a school teacher. She worked like just all get out. And her only fault was that she was with you, if you were in the family, she was with you, right or wrong."

Marshall enjoyed a warm relationship with his parents, but his connection to Aubrey was considerably cooler. The almost four years that separated the two brothers created a natural distance, and Aubrey's interests differed from Thurgood's. Aubrey liked school and nice clothes and got into fights more often than his little brother did. One of Thurgood's classmates once remarked that other than the light skin that both boys shared, they were so different that it was hard to imagine the two were brothers. The gulf between them widened as they got older, and one of Thurgood's roommates later described Aubrey as so irritable, aloof, and serious that he couldn't stand his fun-loving younger brother. "The dislike between Thurgood and Aubrey was so intense . . . I've never seen it in any two brothers that I know who came from the same parents, the same background and everything else."

In 1921 Norma Marshall enrolled in classes at Baltimore's Morgan College to renew her license in preparation for a teaching career. Now that her boys were old enough, she felt ready to follow her family's tradition of working in schools. Her determination to continue her education inspired Thurgood and Aubrey, and it increased the pressure on the brothers to excel. And even though he hadn't finished high school himself, Willie demanded that his sons study hard out of respect for their mother's example—and out of fear of the punishment he'd dish out if they brought home poor grades.

That same year, Marshall entered the Colored High and Training School, later renamed Frederick Douglass High School, and quickly earned a reputation as a goof-off. One high-school classmate recalled, "Thurgood was full of the devil," and sometimes his devilish pranks were aimed at school administrators. One day, for example, Marshall and some of his classmates decided to get even with an assistant principal who had been too tough on them. Marshall instructed one of the girls in his group to go to the assistant principal's office and jump into his lap, timing it so that the other kids would walk into the office to catch him "in the act."

For a cocky teenager like Marshall, growing up in the tough part of town could have led to a life of crime. Even though his parents expected the best of Aubrey and Thurgood, plenty of opportunities for trouble lurked at every turn. Aubrey was considered the favorite child, not just because he was older, but also because he was better looking and better behaved. Everyone who knew him was convinced that of the two Marshall boys, Aubrey would be the one who would amount to something one day. Thurgood may have had more of his father in him. For a short time in his late teens, Thurgood and Willie even worked for a bootlegger on weekends. The illegal booze operation ran its business on an island not far from Baltimore, and Marshall recalled that to get there, they'd "take a motor launch, climb onto a pier, and face a bunch of guys with machine guns and rifles. Boy, was I impressed!" On Sundays the bootleggers also ran a private casino for gangsters and their girlfriends, and Thurgood often saw thousands of dollars won and lost in a single hand of cards. Fortunately, organized crime didn't appeal to Thurgood, and he and his father quit working for the bootleggers before becoming entangled in the business.

His parents, especially his mother, fretted over the fact that he was constantly in trouble at school, but as he got older, there seemed to be little she or most of the teachers could do about it. Eventually the principal came up with a punishment designed to keep the hypertroublemaker out of action for a while. When Marshall was referred to the office for discipline, the principal sent him to the furnace room in the school basement with orders to memorize sections of the U.S. Constitution before he was allowed to come back upstairs. "If you don't think that's terrible," Marshall later told a reporter, "just you try memorizing the Constitution sometime." Neither Marshall nor the principal realized that his frequent constitutional study sessions were preparing him for a legal career founded on constitutional law. "Before I left that school," he said, "I knew the whole thing by heart."

In addition to planning pranks and later paying for them, Marshall managed to absorb the basics of a high-school education. He also developed a greater awareness of racism. His reading of the Constitution helped him realize that the backbone of U.S. law was applied, at best, unevenly among blacks and whites, and his time in one classroom gave him the opportunity to see firsthand how blacks endured injustice at the hands of whites. From his seat near the window of a second-floor classroom, Marshall could see into a local Baltimore police station. The police were all white, but most of the prisoners were black, and some days he saw black prisoners being questioned—and beaten—by white policemen. At times Marshall was so engrossed in scenes of police brutality that the teacher had to order him to close the window blinds. "We could hear police in there," Marshall said, "beating the hell out of people, saying, 'Black boy, why don't you just shut your god-damned mouth, you're going to talk yourself into the electric chair.'"

Despite witnessing the brutal treatment of blacks, Marshall left high school thinking he had a decent education in book learning and in the realities of Jim Crow, but later in life, he would confess, "I didn't get [racism] good until I got to law school. That's when I got it. Up until then, I sort of knew it was there, but law school was when I decided I was going to get something done about it."

# FOUR

## *Roots of Resistance*

**ONE OF THE** best-known stories from Marshall's childhood reveals how his environment and his family's heritage made him a fighter—not a street brawler, but a young man who had the courage to defy racism. He embraced the pride his parents had in their family and their race, and he believed what his father had taught about not taking any guff from anyone. "My father, I mean he told you to stand up for your rights, and no matter what the situation he stood up for his. That's why he lost so many jobs. Most of the time he'd lose 'em or leave 'em, because he was blond and blue-eyed, and every now and then he'd hear somebody say 'nigger,' and there would be an argument, or a fight, and he'd get fired or leave out of pride." Marshall learned from his father's example to stand up for himself, but he also never forgot something his father told him once: "If anyone calls you nigger, you not only got my permission to fight him—you got my orders."

On at least one occasion, Marshall took his father's orders literally.

When he was fifteen, Marshall worked for a Jewish shopkeeper, Mortimer Schoen, owner of a women's clothing store on Pennsylvania Avenue in West Baltimore. Part of Marshall's duties included delivering goods to wealthy customers around town, and on one particularly busy afternoon, Marshall left Schoen's store with a stack of four boxed hats to deliver. Balancing the boxes as best he could, he threaded his way through the busy sidewalk traffic and waited at the curb for a trolley to stop. When a trolley car clanged to a halt in front of him, he peered around his load of boxes to make sure he didn't trip on the steps as he climbed aboard. Concentrating on keeping the stack—and himself—from tumbling over, he bumped into a white woman who was trying to board the trolley at the same time.

Before Marshall realized what he had done, a white man grabbed him by the collar and yanked him from the trolley. "Don't you ever get in front of a white lady," growled the man.

"Damn it," Marshall snapped back, "I'm just trying to get on the damned bus."

Surprised by the cocky reply, the man glared at the teenager and said, "Nigger don't you talk to me like that."

That did it! Marshall dropped the hatboxes and charged into the man with fists flying. The man grabbed Marshall's shirt and tried to wrestle him to the ground, and the two went at it, pushing, punching, and grabbing for advantage, trampling the hats and boxes as they fought. Of course, a crowd quickly formed around the fighters, surprised to see a black teenager standing up to a white man. Before either could finish the other off, a policeman showed up and broke up the fight.

Shaking with exhaustion and rage, Marshall wanted the policeman to listen to both sides, then, after hearing the whole story, to punish the man who had started the fight. But the policeman had seen all he needed to see: a black boy was fighting with a white man, and there could be only one conclusion. Instead of interviewing Marshall, the white man, or bystanders who had seen what happened, the cop arrested Marshall and hauled him down to the local precinct.

At the jailhouse the police allowed Marshall a phone call, so he called Mr. Schoen to tell him about the fight and how the hats had been destroyed. Fortunately, his boss believed Marshall and rushed down to the police station to explain that Marshall hadn't started the fight and to post the fifty-dollar bail to free his teenage employee. As they left the police station, Marshall thanked Mr. Schoen and said, "I'm really sorry that I busted up four of your hats in that fight."

"Was it worth it?" Mr. Schoen asked.

"Sure as hell was," Marshall replied.

"Did he really call you a nigger?"

"Yes, sir, he sure did."

His boss put an arm around Marshall's shoulders and assured him that he had done nothing wrong— and he never asked Marshall to pay him back for the lost hats.

Marshall considered his fighting spirit a part of his heritage, and he often repeated a family story about one of his great-grandfathers, perhaps the root of the

*Marshall as a teenager.*

family's toughness. Apparently, some of the "snooty" members of his family wanted to believe that the great-grandfather had descended from a sophisticated tribe in Sierra Leone, West Africa. Marshall knew otherwise, and he once told a friend,

> He really came from the toughest part of the Congo. A big-game hunting family had picked up my great-grandfather on one of their safaris into the Congo and brought him back to the Eastern Shore of Maryland—only to find that this black man didn't cotton to the idea of slavery. He expressed his objections so rebelliously that one day the slavemaster said to him:
>
> "Look: I brought you here, so I guess I can't shoot you, which is what you deserve. I can't in good conscience sell anyone as vicious as you to another slaveholder. So I'm gonna set you free on one condition: You get the hell out of this county and never set foot here again."

Annie Marshall, Thurgood's grandmother, carried on the family's tradition of fearlessness in the face of unrighteous authority. At least one writer believes that she may have been the first American to have used the sit-down strike as a form of protest. Family history says that one day the electric company in Baltimore announced plans to install a utility pole on the sidewalk right in front of the Marshalls' grocery store. Annie protested, but a black woman in those days had no voice in legal matters, so a judge ruled that the company could go ahead and install the pole. When she realized that the city would not protect her rights, Annie Marshall took one of her kitchen chairs out to the sidewalk and placed it exactly over the spot marked for the pole. She sat there for days, daring the electric workers to just try to make her move. Her family had paid for that sidewalk, she said, and no one had the right to plant a pole in it.

Her protest worked, and the electric company finally decided that it could find a better place to locate a utility pole.

Marshall's mother's family also contributed to his heritage of resistance. His mother's mother had inspired him with stories about the early black activists like Frederick Douglass, but his mother's father inspired Marshall by example. After the Civil War, Isaiah O. B. Williams had traveled the world with the United States Navy before returning to Baltimore to settle down and start a family. His navy experiences had convinced him that as a free man, he deserved to be treated just like any other citizen, so he purchased a house in a poor integrated West Baltimore neighborhood filled with recent European immigrants and freed blacks. He lived, worked, and attended a white church in that neighborhood, and he never backed down from a fight.

One of his neighbors was a German man with a reputation for being hard to get along with. He'd probably had several confrontations with people in the neighborhood, including Isaiah, but one day he came to Isaiah concerned about the broken-down fence that separated their properties. The fence needed mending, the German neighbor told Isaiah, and they shouldn't let race keep them from taking care of the problem. "After all," the neighbor explained, "we belong to the same church and are going to the same heaven."

"I'd rather go to hell," Isaiah replied.

This same grandfather established a tradition of

defending the rights of blacks long before there were any laws or civil-rights organizations to help him. The best-documented example of this occurred on July 31, 1875, when police responded to complaints of a loud party in a neighborhood a few blocks from Isaiah's home. When a policeman ordered the crowd to quiet down, the mood of the party turned ugly, and one of the black men, Daniel Brown, argued with the officer, got clubbed, then was shot in the head.

Isaiah led a protest against the police brutality, and at a rally held in the Douglass Institute in Baltimore pointed out the racial problems that plagued the city in 1875. "There is little protection, if any," he said, "afforded us by the police in cases of assault where the offenders are white." A local paper reported that the crowd warmed to Isaiah's speech, especially when he told them that the black citizens of Baltimore only wanted justice, "and the same protections in life, liberty and the pursuit of happiness which white men enjoy as a right."

The political pressure brought by Isaiah and a handful of other black activists forced the city to investigate the killing and eventually to put the policeman on trial. As a black man, Isaiah wasn't allowed to testify, but he attended the trial as often as he could and was in the front of the courtroom on November 22 when the lawyers made their closing arguments. The next day, the jury convicted the policeman not of murder, as Isaiah and others had hoped, but of manslaughter. Given the circumstances, Isaiah and his supporters considered the verdict a huge victory. Years later this story provided Marshall's family with another example of how courage and activism could overcome racism and inequality.

As he grew older, Marshall realized that even though these stories ennobled his family's long struggle against racial injustice, the struggle came at a cost. "I later learned that often my father would take a walk and come home furious" because of racist signs he had seen in the city. The frustrations and abuse created by an overwhelmingly racist society took a toll on the entire family, but especially on Marshall's father. Recalling his childhood, Marshall told an interviewer, "My father was castrated mentally and emotionally by the bigots who controlled employment and almost all other aspects of life in and around Baltimore."

Marshall managed to control his fighting spirit and his tendency to goof off well enough that in 1925 he was able to graduate from high school a semester early. No doubt weary from trying to contain the trouble-maker Marshall for three and a half years, Frederick Douglass High School's principal, Mason Hawkins, was glad to see him graduate, and he recommended Marshall as a student with "very good ability."

Hoping to further his education—and, most likely, to get away from home for a while—Marshall decided to follow in the footsteps of his older brother, Aubrey, and applied to Lincoln University, a small male-only private black college near Oxford, Pennsylvania. His parents had always expected him to become a dentist, so Marshall planned to enroll in the predental pro-gram even though he really wasn't sure what career he wanted to pursue.

# FIVE

## *Easing Along*

**LINCOLN UNIVERSITY ACCEPTED** the brash kid from Baltimore, but acceptance didn't guarantee attendance. Because Aubrey Marshall had fallen behind in his tuition payments, school officials worried that Thurgood also might run into financial troubles, so they recommended that he work for a year before enrolling. Marshall had been working as a dining-car waiter for the local railroad, but he couldn't convince the school that he'd be able to finance his college education. Fortunately, a family friend and Lincoln alumnus wrote a letter encouraging the school to allow him to enroll on time. The school agreed, and Marshall moved to Oxford, Pennsylvania, and started classes in September 1925.

Marshall dove into college life like a boy gone wild.

*A 1930s photograph of Rendell Hall, a building at the center of Lincoln University's campus.*

He joined a fraternity, made the varsity debating team as a freshman, and became known as a campus prankster. Fraternity life suited him, and he quickly earned a reputation as a kid who never studied, spending his time instead in smoke-filled dormitory rooms playing cards, reading comic books, or talking about girls. He loved parties and cowboy movies, and his friends assumed that he filled his days—and nights—with fun. One of his classmates reported that Marshall's dorm room hosted nonstop parties, and another friend recalled that Marshall was easily the loudest guy in the dorms, and given his preference for parties over study, "the least likely to succeed." Somehow, though, Marshall avoided flunking out of school his freshman year.

Grades, it turned out, were the least of his worries. Though his fraternity brothers and classmates believed that Marshall never studied, he did just enough to stay in school. Most of his trouble at Lincoln came from the goof-off personality he had developed in high school. "He was suspended, or on the verge of being thrown out of Lincoln every year," recalled an adult acquaintance. "He was accused of being involved in drunken celebrations after football games, of hazing underclassmen viciously, of leading a strike for better food." His bad-boy behavior finally caught up with him after a prank gone out of control: Marshall and some of his fraternity buddies shaved the heads of a group of freshmen, then paddled them without mercy—and the university suspended Marshall and his friends. That would have been the end of Marshall's career at Lincoln if an upperclassman, the famous African American poet Langston Hughes, hadn't convinced the administration to give the boys a second chance.

Throughout his time at Lincoln, Marshall

worked hard to earn money for books, tuition, living expenses—and parties. One of his jobs was working in the campus bakery that made bread, pies, and
cakes for the students. Marshall especially liked the
bread, even though, by today's standards, it would
be rejected because he and the other young men who
kneaded the bread dough worked without shirts, and
sweated profusely in the oven heat of the bakery.
"They didn't need to put salt in the bread," he said.
"The sweat took care of that."

During the summers, Marshall worked as a waiter at
the Gibson Island Club, an upscale whites-only country club on Chesapeake Bay, where his father worked as
head steward. As a bright, friendly, and light-skinned
young African American, Marshall turned out to be
a popular waiter, and the tips added significantly to
his hourly wages. The job allowed Marshall to earn
enough money for college tuition, but it also subjected
him to the kind of racist treatment his father had endured all his life. One incident in particular stood out
in Marshall's memory: Marshall waited on the table
of a U.S. senator who was a member of the club, and
the senator antagonized the young college student by

calling him "nigger" and "boy" throughout the meal. Marshall endured the humiliating racist treatment because he knew he couldn't afford to lose his job or cause trouble for his father.

At the end of the dinner, the senator stunned Marshall by leaving a twenty-dollar tip—almost a week's earnings! The senator dined at the club the next night and every night for a week, each time insisting that Marshall be his waiter and each time calling him racist names yet leaving a mind-boggling twenty-dollar tip.

Marshall's father nearly ruined the financial windfall one night when he saw Thurgood meekly serving the senator despite the man's racist language. Infuriated at his son's willingness to put up with such insults, he pulled Thurgood aside and told him, "You are fired! You're a disgrace to the colored people!"

Marshall calmed his father down, explaining that he didn't mind the senator's racist talk as long as he kept paying such huge tips. "I figure it's worth about twenty dollars to be called nigger," he said, and then he reassured his father that he hadn't forgotten his family's stance on tolerating racism. He told his father that while putting up with the senator's abuse, Marshall was thinking, *But the minute you run out of them twenties . . . I'm gonna bust you in the nose.*

The country club job provided enough income to keep Marshall in school pursuing fun full-time and academics part-time. He'd gone to Lincoln with the lukewarm intention of becoming a dentist because that's what his parents expected. They knew, of course, that he wouldn't be allowed to work with white patients, but dentistry would be a stable job that would guarantee a comfortable life for Marshall and his family. As a predental major, he had to take classes in the sciences, but once again his wisecracking frat-boy attitude got him into trouble, and this trouble changed the course of his college career—and his life.

All the professors at Lincoln University were white, and Marshall respected most of them, but after making an off-color wisecrack in one predental science class, he "had great trouble with the professor— he and I had a mutual dislike for each other—so I gave that up, and went into the social sciences under Professor Larabee." Recalling the career-changing event many years later, Marshall told an interviewer,

"At times I think I'm sorry . . . I could have made a lot more money as a dentist. Then I tell myself I'm glad. Hell, my hands are too big to put in somebody's mouth."

Some of the most valuable lessons Marshall learned during his time at Lincoln came not in the classroom but in the segregated world off campus. Like most towns in America, segregation laws applied in Oxford, Pennsylvania, and that meant that the students from Lincoln confronted racism almost every time they went into town. Perhaps because he was preoccupied with the fun of his all-black college, the obviously unfair treatment in town—and at times, even on campus—didn't seem to bother Marshall. In fact, when a group of students demanded that the university include African Americans on the Lincoln faculty, Marshall joined the majority that voted to keep the faculty all white.

Like most of his fellow students, Marshall believed that African American professors would favor one fraternity over the other and that would lead to favoritism in classes and grading. The students also accepted the notion that "if it ain't broke, don't fix it."

Lincoln University had been doing fine for years with an all-white faculty, so there was no reason to change. Langston Hughes, one of the leaders in the fight for integration, said that the third reason for keeping the faculty white was the strangest of all: most students believed that black students wouldn't cooperate with black teachers. Marshall accepted these arguments, but not because he'd thought about them; he simply went along with the crowd.

Marshall realized he could no longer go along with the crowd one Saturday afternoon when he and some friends went into Oxford to see a movie. They bought tickets and tried to enter the main theater, but an usher told them they couldn't sit there; African Americans had to sit in the "colored section" in the balcony. The Lincoln students ignored the usher, sat in the white section, and settled in to enjoy the movie. Not long after the movie started, however, someone in the darkened theater yelled, "Nigger, why don't you just get out of here and sit where you belong?" Marshall shot back that he and his friends had purchased tickets just like everyone else, and they didn't intend to give up their seats. An argument followed, and the Lincoln students finally got up, tore down a set of curtains, and left the theater—breaking the front door on their way—hoping that no angry whites or police would catch them.

It turned out that they didn't need to worry. "We found out that they only had one fat cop in the whole town," Marshall later wrote to his parents, "and they wouldn't have the nerve or the room to arrest all of us. But the amazing thing was that when we were leaving, we just walked out with all those people and they didn't do anything, didn't say anything, didn't even look at us. . . . I'm not sure I like being invisible, but maybe it's better than being put to shame and not able to respect yourself."

The experience in the movie theater awoke in Marshall a greater awareness of the effects of racism and reminded him how good it felt to stand up against oppression. "We desegregated the theatre in the little town of Oxford," he said. "I guess that's what started the whole thing in my life."

Of course, the experience didn't trigger an immediate change in Marshall the frat boy. He continued staying up late, drinking, playing cards, and chasing women. Tall and handsome, Marshall was popular with young women, so popular that by the time he graduated, he had been engaged "at least nine times." As he got older, his study habits didn't change much. "I just eased along," he said, "you know, do good enough to pass"—but as he neared graduation, he began to outgrow his playboy, party image.

When he was twenty, Marshall finally fell in love. Lincoln University urged all students to attend church on weekends, so Marshall and some friends often attended services at Cherry Street Memorial Church in Philadelphia, not for spiritual enlightenment but, as Marshall said, "because we learned that's where all the cute chicks went." At one of the church meetings, Marshall met Vivian "Buster" Burey, an attractive student from the University of Pennsylvania. (Years later, Marshall would claim that they met at an ice cream parlor in Philadelphia; Buster said they had met much earlier, but Marshall didn't remember meeting her because "he was so busy arguing and debating with everyone at the table.")

What made Buster stand out from all the other girls Marshall had been chasing? Her physical appearance first caught his eye. Marshall and his college buddies relied on a rating system to determine a young woman's attractiveness. "First," Marshall said, "you look at a gal's ankles, and they if are attractive, you look at her legs," and so on. "She had everything. She wasn't beautiful. No way all that beautiful. But she was put together nicely—black hair, black eyes, and *very nice*. She got along with me." Perhaps Buster offered Marshall what he needed most: someone who could get along with him.

They began dating on the weekends, fell in love, and started talking marriage. At first, said Marshall, "We decided to get married five years after I graduated, then three, then one, and we finally did, just before I started my last semester."

Marshall and his wife were both twenty-one when they got married in the Cherry Street Memorial Church on September 4, 1929, and Buster's influence helped transform him from a party boy to a serious student. Despite his previous history of lax studies and loud parties, in January 1930, Marshall not only graduated but also managed "to be on the honor list, even though I was the last one on there."

# SIX

## *Digging Deep into Law*

**MARSHALL'S EXPERIENCE AT** Lincoln University convinced him that he wanted to attend law school, a decision that, in retrospect, is not all that surprising. He and Buster had previously discussed his career options. Teaching was a respectable possibility, but it didn't pay well. They considered the ministry, but Marshall's temperament and the low salaries eliminated that profession. Dentistry, Marshall's original career choice, was no longer an option. Given the couple's hopes for a good salary, prestige, and a career that suited Marshall's personality and skills, they decided that he should become a lawyer.

One reporter suggested that Marshall's career in law came from the fact that he "seems to have majored in arguing and hellraising in Pennsylvania." While that may be true, his family also had considerable influence on his decision. For much of his life, Marshall's father found that observing trials in Baltimore provided a nice change of pace from his menial work as a railroad porter and then as a steward at the Gibson Island Club. When he came home at night, he'd tell Thurgood and Aubrey about what he had seen in the courtrooms. He'd also act like a lawyer during the dinnertime discussions with his sons.

Later in his career, Marshall pointed to those discussions as the beginnings of his interest in the legal profession. He told one reporter, "My dad, my brother, and I had the most violent arguments you ever heard about anything. I guess we argued five nights out of seven at the dinner table. When we were away at college, and we would come back, the first dinner we'd have—I remember a neighbor of ours, Mrs. Hall, would tell her husband, 'Ah the boys are home.' She could hear it through the walls."

The arguments around the dinner table were boot camp for the courtroom. "Oh yes," said Marshall, "we talked about the law. . . . We fussed about it and argued and carried on." He recalled, "My father never told me to become a lawyer. But he turned me into one by teaching me to argue, to prove every statement I made, and by challenging my logic on every point."

After graduation, Marshall and his new bride moved to his parents' home in Baltimore, and he resumed his job as a waiter at Gibson Island. Living at home would help the newlyweds save money for Marshall's tuition, and it would also make life and law school more convenient. Marshall had decided to study law at the University of Maryland, where he would be able to pay in-state tuition and have an easy commute to the university's campus in downtown Baltimore.

Unfortunately, the state university rejected Marshall's application. The University of Maryland Law School had never had any African American students, and they weren't about to make Thurgood Marshall their first.

The racist rejection enraged Marshall, but he knew there was nothing he could do about it. He swallowed his pride and applied for admission to the law school at Howard University, an African American college in Washington, D.C., sometimes known as the "dummy's retreat," said Marshall, "because the only people who went there were those who couldn't get into any other school." Though the university had a poor reputation, the Howard University School of Law had a long tradition of preparing African American lawyers. Its first classes began in 1869, and in 1872, it had the distinction of graduating the first black woman to practice law in the United States, Charlotte E. Ray.

The law school accepted Marshall almost immediately, and he resigned himself to going there, but even after several months of work at Gibson Island, he still didn't have enough money for tuition. With no other option for law school, he decided to delay for a year to save up the money. When his mother heard about his decision, she told him she wouldn't allow it. "You're going," she said. "I'll pawn my engagement and wedding rings to help you." The rings brought enough cash for tuition, and Marshall was off to Howard in the fall of 1930.

Law school demanded everything Marshall could give. He had to leave Baltimore at 5:30 a.m. for the forty-mile train ride to Washington. Classes kept him busy until 3:00 each afternoon, and then he would take the train back to Baltimore, where he worked a part-time job, after which he would study until midnight. Fortunately he was up to the grueling schedule, and he became a top student, studying law books in the segregated train cars to and from school and concentrating in class like never before. He wanted to make the most of his chance to study law, and after all his years of goofing off, he was ready to work. "I'd got the horsin' around out of my system, and I'd heard lawbooks were to dig in. So I dug, way deep."

At Howard, Marshall's most demanding—and influential—professor was Charles Hamilton Houston, a prominent African American, Harvard-trained lawyer, and the first African American to argue a case before the U.S. Supreme Court. Houston's intensity and high expectations helped transform Marshall from a happy-go-lucky undergraduate into a serious law student. That first day in class, Professor Houston surveyed his first-year students and instead of welcoming them, issued this warning: "Every man here look at the man on your left. Now look at the man on your right. This time next year, two of you won't be here. . . . I'll never be satisfied until I go to one of the dances up on the hill on the campus and see

*Charles Hamilton Houston presents a brief to a government agency in the 1930s.*

everybody having fun with all my law school students sitting around the sides reading law books. . . . Then I'll be happy, and not before." His announcement shocked the entire class. Even the hardworking, gifted students were worried because Professor Houston added, "The only thing I love is to flunk valedictorians and smart people."

Houston became Marshall's favorite professor and mentor, who inspired his protégé to reach new heights.

"I never worked hard until I got to the Howard Law School and met Charlie Houston," Marshall said years later. "I saw this man's dedication, his vision, his willingness to sacrifice, and I told myself, 'You either shape up or ship out.' When you are being challenged by a great human being, you know that you can't ship out."

Houston enriched his classes by bringing in some of the most famous lawyers in America: Clarence Darrow from the famous Scopes monkey trial; future Supreme Court justice Felix Frankfurter; John W. Davis, former solicitor general of the United States, and other leaders in the legal profession. In addition to outstanding guest speakers, Houston also provided experiences that stretched his students' understanding of the effects of the legal system on private citizens. On Saturdays he would take them on field trips to police stations, prisons, courtrooms, even an insane asylum. One of the most memorable excursions took the law students to witness an autopsy, and it's a story that Marshall loved to retell: "We went to that autopsy, and the doctor that performed it was the coroner himself. And he says, 'Now some of you better watch out—hold onto something—'cause you're gonna fall.' And he slit the guy down here—like this—and rolled his skin down like a windowshade. By this time, all of us were laying down on the floor."

Houston encouraged his students to make field trips of their own, so Marshall attended trials when he could, including trials held at the U.S. Supreme Court. He learned much about strategy and law from his courtroom observations, but he was most inspired by John W. Davis, a "lawyer's lawyer" who had argued more cases before the Supreme Court than anyone in U.S. history. In addition to Davis's unparalleled record as a lawyer, Marshall admired his courtroom style and especially his profound respect for the law. "Any lawyer who [trims] his professional course to fit the gusts of popular opinion," Davis once said, "degrades the great profession." To the young Marshall, John W. Davis represented everything he hoped to become.

Whenever Davis appeared before the Supreme Court, Marshall would skip classes to observe the master lawyer in action. The awestruck law student often wondered if one day he himself might have the privilege of presenting a case to the highest court in the land. At the time, that dream seemed not merely ambitious, but impossible. "Every time John Davis argued, I'd ask myself, 'Will I ever, ever . . . ?' and every time I had to answer, 'No never.'"

But the field trips, the guest speakers, even the intense lectures were only part of the education Houston's students received. Perhaps the richest learning came from the demands he placed on each student. Houston was a perfectionist, and he expected his students to be perfect as well. Marshall said that "[what] Charlie beat into our heads was excellence." The law professor made it clear that it was the students' responsibility to make the most of their education. The legal system, like Houston, would make no allowance for a poorly prepared lawyer. In one lecture he reminded students that "when you get in a courtroom, you can't just say, 'Please Mr. Court, have mercy on me because I'm a Negro.' You are in competition with a well-trained white lawyer, and you better be better. If I give you five cases to read overnight, you better read eight. And when I say eight, you read ten. You go that step further, and you might make it." He drilled into his students that nothing could make up for hard work and thorough preparation: "You've got to go out and compete with the other man, and you've got to be better than he is. You might never get what you deserve, but you'll certainly *not* get what you *don't* deserve."

Marshall and a handful of classmates fell in line with their hard-driving professor and dug deep into their studies. In addition to accepting Houston's work ethic, they also bought into his legal philosophy. Harvard University, Houston told them, trained lawyers to work for corporations, but he trained lawyers to do battle in court. Marshall said that Houston made it clear that he wanted his students to "be social engineers rather than lawyers. And I had early decided that's what I wanted to do." Houston wanted to train first-rate lawyers, but he expected his graduates to use their legal skills to make a difference in the world, especially a difference for African Americans. In one class discussion about racism and segregation, Houston told his students, "We've got to turn this whole thing around. And the black man has got to do it; nobody's going to do it for you."

Marshall made up his mind to do exactly that: "turn this whole thing around."

# SEVEN

## A Hungry Young Lawyer

**IN THE SPRING** of 1933, Thurgood Marshall graduated as valedictorian from Howard University School of Law. That fall he passed the Maryland state bar examination, earning his license to practice law, and set off on his new career with the idealism and enthusiasm of a schoolboy on the first day of summer vacation.

Marshall rented a small office on the sixth floor of the Phoenix Building in Baltimore, hired a secretary for $7.50 a week, and waited for work to come in. Unfortunately, business was excruciatingly slow. Though well-schooled in law and the practice of it, Marshall had no experience earning a living as a lawyer, and in his first year on the job, his law practice lost $3,500.

His financial losses were no surprise. America

wallowed in the worst economic depression in history; unemployment, especially among African Americans, choked the nation, and many of the people who had jobs worked for goods, not cash. Few of the clients who hired Marshall had much money, and the most desperate cases, the ones he often had the most interest in, almost never involved any significant fee. When a poor African American came in for legal help, especially if the help involved protecting his civil rights, Marshall would take the case for free.

Unfortunately, free wasn't always good enough to attract potential clients. Because whites dominated the legal system in Baltimore, some African Americans feared trusting their legal fates to African American lawyers. In the 1920s and 1930s black colleges had a reputation for preparing poorly qualified professionals, so some African Americans lived by the saying, "If you want to die, go to a black doctor; if you want to go to jail, go to a black lawyer."

With few clients and sporadic income, working conditions were difficult for Marshall and his secretary, but she remained loyal to her boss. Marshall, she once said, "had a genius for ignoring cases that might earn him any money. Sometimes we'd get our $7.50 a week, sometimes we'd just get carfare, other times we were out-of-pocket at the end of the week. But we loved that man." Early in his career, money was so scarce that Marshall and his secretary had to share their lunches from home. "She would bring lunch for two one day," he said, "and I'd bring lunch for two the next day, and that's the way we lived. . . . Sometimes, we'd be the only two people in that office for weeks at a time." Times were hard, but it wasn't always leftovers and sandwiches. "Once in a while," Marshall recalled, "I got a good fee. Then my secretary would immediately take the check to the bank. She'd call her husband and I'd call Buster, and we'd get the biggest steak in town to celebrate."

In that first year, however, such celebrations were rare, and Marshall struggled to make a living. He'd taken a risk by opening his own office, and at times he worried that he might have made a terrible mistake. "I bought some fancy stationery that made me look like a hugely successful lawyer when I didn't have a damn dollar to pay for it. I would close out one telephone number and open another account when I couldn't pay the bill. Hell, how can you be a big-time lawyer if you don't have a telephone number?"

The struggling U.S. economy dried up the wallets of many potential clients, and the pervasive Jim Crow culture piled on more problems for Marshall. Even though he had graduated from law school and passed the state bar exam, Marshall, like other African American lawyers in Maryland, could not join the local bar association and was thus prevented from using its law library. That severely limited his opportunities to do the legal research necessary to prepare for trials. The tiny office in the Phoenix Building had few law books, and Marshall had neither the time nor the money to travel to Howard University regularly for research. He finally solved the problem by using the training he'd received from Charles Houston. Marshall recalled that the local bar association "wouldn't admit Negroes. And they had a very good library in Baltimore at the bar association. But it was housed in the courthouse. And we raised the point and the court ruled that they had to let us in whether we were members of the bar or not. Because it was in the courthouse. So we got it for free. They had to pay and we didn't."

Marshall's struggles continued. A few cases came his way now and then, and he resigned himself to accepting work ranging from traffic violations to misdemeanor criminal cases. He didn't earn much money, but he gained valuable courtroom experience, nearly always working against better-paid white lawyers arguing cases before white judges. Marshall had his share of success, but because he was "colored," the white lawyers and judges didn't treat him with the professional courtesy expected of men engaged in the practice of law. Exasperated by the disrespect, Marshall finally turned to Warner McGuinn, a Yale graduate and Baltimore's most prominent African American lawyer, for advice.

> I said one day, "Mr. McGuinn, I've got a problem. These white lawyers, they run into me in the hall and call me by my first name. Why can't they call me Mister like everybody else?"
>
> "No problem," he said.
>
> "What do you mean?" I said.
>
> "Make it your order of business that whenever a white man calls you by your first name,

go straight to the phone book, find his first name and the next time you see him, call him by his first name," he said.

And it worked.

Marshall's courage in confronting racism and his courtroom successes quickly earned him a reputation as the people's lawyer, a man willing to defend African Americans, to take a case—free if necessary—on behalf of Baltimore's poorest citizens. His reputation attracted more clients, some of whom expected him to work for free. For a while, Marshall didn't mind the occasional pro bono work, but as he gained experience, he realized that taking cases for free "wasn't a good way to make a living." With a wife to provide for and an office to maintain, Marshall knew he had to find a way to generate a regular income.

The turning point came one day early in his career in Baltimore. An old African American woman from North Carolina shuffled into his office looking for a lawyer. When Marshall asked her if she had any money to pay his fees, she told him, "I don't have a nickel."

"What are you coming to me for?" he asked.

"Well," she said, "down in North Carolina in my little town, when we have a legal problem, we go to the judge and he helps us out, so I asked for the [Baltimore] court house and I went down there and I walked into the judges' chambers and told him. And he said he was sorry, but they didn't do things that way in Baltimore."

When the woman had told the judge she didn't have any money, he'd replied, "Well, that's a problem. But I tell you what—you go down to this lawyer Thurgood Marshall at 4 East Redwood Street . . . He's a freebie lawyer; he'll do it for you for nothing."

Marshall later said, "It was all those freebies that finally sent me to the NAACP."

In 1934 Marshall accepted some cases on behalf of the Baltimore branch of the National Association for the Advancement of Colored People (NAACP), the leading civil-rights organization in America, to gain courtroom experience. One of his first assignments was organizing a boycott of white-owned stores in black neighborhoods, stores that served African American customers but refused to hire African American employees. The boycott was successful, so successful that the store owners sued the NAACP for damaging their businesses. Given the assignment to defend the NAACP in the case, Marshall invited Charles Houston to help. Marshall did the legal research, Houston argued the case in Baltimore federal court, and the pair won the trial. The victory whetted Marshall's appetite for civil-rights work, and with the local NAACP behind him, he became even more involved in the legal struggle for civil rights. He lobbied Maryland congressmen to support federal antilynching laws, he saved an African American murder suspect from the death penalty, he forced local country clubs to allow African Americans to play on their golf courses, and he began the battle for equal pay for Maryland's black schoolteachers, most of whom earned less than half of what white teachers made.

Marshall's successes for the Baltimore group earned him respect and experience but little money. The underfunded NAACP chapter continued to call him in on cases, even though Lillie May Jackson, one of its board members, didn't approve of Marshall's wild ways. She was upset that whenever Roy Wilkins from the national NAACP visited Baltimore, Marshall and Wilkins would spend much of their free time drinking at jazz joints. When Jackson complained that Marshall's behavior hurt the organization's reputation, he told her that his drinking and smoking habits were his business, not hers. "Start paying me some salary," he said, "and I will think about listening to you. But you don't pay me a goddamn nickel, then you want to run my life. You can't do 'em both."

While Marshall struggled to earn a living in Baltimore, Charles Houston had left Howard University and begun working as a special legal consultant for the NAACP main office. Since 1909 the NAACP had focused its energies on protecting the legal rights of African Americans, and it spent most of its time defending African Americans in unfair trials and working to dismantle racial segregation. Houston despised segregation, and he wanted to attack Jim Crow at its weakest point: schools. He planned to use the *Plessy v. Ferguson* separate but equal principle and the Fourteenth Amendment's "equal protection of the laws" provision to demand equal educational opportunity for African Americans. First he had to document that black schools truly were inequitable, so he made regular trips to the South to observe the terrible conditions in black schools. Houston sometimes invited Marshall to join him on his research trips. The long hours they spent traveling the South gave them plenty of time to discuss segregation, constitutional law, and legal strategy, and also cemented the professional relationship between the two men and convinced Marshall that now was the time to attack Jim Crow.

Marshall didn't have to look very far to find a case. "My first idea," he said, "was to get even with the University of Maryland for not letting me into its law school." Marshall had heard that a group of lawyers was considering suing the university for its racist admission policies, so he wrote Charles Houston and asked to be allowed to be the first to file suit. Houston gave Marshall permission and encouraged him to start on the case. Not wanting to use his own experience with the University of Maryland as the basis for the lawsuit, Marshall began searching for a suitable plaintiff, an African American qualified for admission to the law school.

At the end of 1934 Marshall discovered Donald Gaines Murray, a graduate of Amherst College and a member of a highly respected African American family in Baltimore. Murray had an interest in applying

*Marshall, standing, with Donald Murray and Charles Houston as they prepare for their case against the University of Maryland.*

to law school, and Marshall convinced him to apply to the University of Maryland. His inevitable rejection would provide the basis for a lawsuit against the school.

Murray applied, the law school rejected his application, and Marshall filed suit in Baltimore court, demanding that Murray be admitted to the state law school.

With the case now under way, Charles Houston

joined the action, bringing with him support from the NAACP headquarters and serving as the lead attorney with Marshall as his assistant. Marshall welcomed the opportunity to work with Houston on what might be an important civil-rights case. Before the trial could begin, he had to attend the pretrial hearings that would determine a trial date. Marshall's more experienced opponent, Maryland's assistant attorney general, used one technicality after another to delay the trial, and Marshall felt helpless to stop him. He knew that he could object to the attorney general's requests, but he worried that doing so might alienate the white judge, and he desperately wanted the judge to give the trial a fair chance.

What happened next was something Marshall would never forget.

One day I came into court, and they had moved for an adjournment, and Judge O'Dunne sent for me and said, "Look, do you want to try this case or not?"

I said, "Yes, sir, of course I do."

He said, "Well, act like it."

I said, "What do you mean by that?"

He said, "When the attorney general asks for adjournment, object."

I said, "Is that—?"

He said, "Sure, that's all you have to do."

So [the attorney general] came in and said he wanted it, expecting me to jump up and say "No objection." I said, "I object."

Judge O'Dunne said, "We'll start trying this tomorrow."

In court the next morning, Houston and Marshall argued that the University of Maryland's racist admission policy violated the constitutional guarantee of equal protection. Maryland did not have a separate—and equal—law school for its African American residents; additionally, the school's admissions policies specifically prohibited African Americans—but no other racial minorities—from enrolling. Because of this, the University of Maryland should be ordered to admit Murray—and any other qualified African American applicant—to its law school. Houston hammered home his point, calling in one university administrator after another to prove that the law school discriminated against African American applicants and, in so doing, damaged the applicants' opportunity to practice law successfully in the state of Maryland. Marshall watched the master at work, and when Houston had hacked away at all the university's defenses, took over for the closing argument. Knowing how much depended on this case, he must have been nervous addressing the white judge in the crowded courtroom.

Taking a deep breath, Marshall summarized the key points of the case and concluded by reminding the judge that the state's commitment to the Constitution, not racism, was on trial. "What's at stake is more than just the rights of my client," he said. "It is the moral commitment stated in our country's creed."

Marshall had expected the trial to be long and complicated and assumed that he and Houston would lose the case, so he had begun preparing for an appeal that, with luck, would take the case all the way to the Supreme Court. To everyone's surprise, however, after only four days of argument, Judge O'Dunne ended the case, ruling that the University of Maryland had to admit Donald Gaines Murray to its law school.

Immediately.

The unexpected and sudden victory stunned the lawyers and ignited celebrations citywide. One NAACP worker said that Marshall's success in the case "set the colored people in Baltimore on fire. They were euphoric with victory. . . . We didn't know about the Constitution. [Marshall] brought us the Constitution like Moses brought the people the Ten Command-ments." Marshall celebrated the victory with Hous-ton but was quick to give the credit to his mentor. "I worked the case out on the ground," he told reporters, "and I drew the pleadings since there was some intri-cate old Maryland common law involved, but outside the legwork, I did very little. The court presentation was [Houston's] doing." Black newspapers trumpeted the legal triumph, and the national NAACP and Af-rican Americans around the nation began to see a flicker of hope in the dark cloud of segregation that had hung over them for centuries.

Nobody at the time knew that Thurgood Marshall was just getting started.

# EIGHT

## *Taking Jim Crow to Court*

**ENCOURAGED BY HIS** success in the *Murray* case
and by his association with Charles Houston, Marshall
continued his courtroom apprenticeship, taking cases
that taught him how to wield the law in defense of
African American victims of discrimination and
racism. In the same year he argued the celebrated
*Murray* case, he also lost an important case, and
that loss motivated him to work harder than ever to
protect the rights of African Americans in court.

A neighbor of Marshall's had convinced him to defend James Gross, one of three young men accused of
robbery and murder at a barbecue shop in Maryland.
At the trial, Marshall tried to convince the court that
because Gross had merely been an accomplice—he
drove the getaway vehicle—he should not be charged
with first-degree murder. The judge disagreed and sen-

tenced all three men to death by hanging. Before the sentence could be carried out, however, one of the men, Donald Parker—the man Marshall considered to be the ringleader—had his sentence changed from death to life in prison.

James Gross died on the gallows.

The loss stung Marshall, not only because the state had executed his client, but because his inexperience may have been a factor in the defeat. Said the neighbor who had convinced Marshall to take the case, "The ringleader got off—he had a smarter lawyer than what the other boys had at the time. . . . Parker's lawyers were white." The devastating defeat inspired Marshall to throw himself into his work with even greater devotion.

His new determination paid off. Not long after the James Gross trial, Marshall defended Virtis Lucas, another African American accused of murdering a white man. Marshall's pretrial research provided enough evidence to help him convince the white judge and jury that his client could not have been the killer. The court reduced the charge, and Lucas served only six months in jail.

Marshall's growing reputation as a civil-rights

lawyer provided the stepping stone he needed to move from a poorly paid private practice to more secure employment, a job that would provide a steady income and allow him to devote all his energy to attacking Jim Crow.

"I got the break of my lifetime," Marshall said.

Charlie Houston called in 1936 to ask me to come to New York as his deputy, as assistant special counsel of the national NAACP. He said he would pay me twenty-four hundred dollars a year. I whooped and hollered so loud that Buster ran in to see if I was dying. . . . Buster and I wouldn't have to live with my parents anymore. We gathered up our rags and moved to New York, where we rented a little apartment near the Polo Grounds.

But it was more than just the job security that thrilled Marshall about this new opportunity. "I felt that I suddenly had a real chance to do something to end Jim Crow."

Houston and Marshall would become powerful but

unusual allies. "Charles Hamilton Houston was a fairly formal person," said one law professor. "Thurgood Marshall was a loud, liquor-drinking, chain-smoking, take-life-easy sort of person. I mean, they seemed to have been the quintessential odd couple. But what they had in common was they both were brilliant, they both were willing to work hard, and they both were courageous."

The NAACP headquarters in New York impressed Marshall. After working in a shoe box–sized office in Baltimore, Marshall considered the NAACP offices incredibly spacious, but the Charles Houston formality felt too confining. "How very tush-tush," he complained. "It was Dr. Whosis and Mr. Whatsis and all kind of nonsense like that, bowing and scraping like an embassy scene." Marshall knew that had to change. "Well, I took a long look . . . not too long but long enough and I figured I'd have to bust that stuff up pretty quick. Believe me, I had 'em talking first names in nothin' time and no more of that formality business. I was gonna relax and operate in my natural-born way and that's just what happened."

In his new position, Marshall had the time and

resources to focus on civil-rights cases, and with Houston's help, he began to craft a legal strategy for defeating segregation. He took on several criminal cases, usually defending African American clients who had been falsely accused or received unfair trials, but in September 1935, Marshall received a letter that gave him a case similar to the NAACP's victory against the University of Maryland and put him back on track to attack segregation in public education.

Lloyd L. Gaines, an African American graduate of a black college in Missouri, wanted to attend law school at the University of Missouri but knew that the school's racist policies would prevent him from doing so. In his letter to the NAACP, Gaines wrote, "I am appealing to you in the name of social justice, to back my efforts to receive my rightful consideration. May I rely upon your assistance at such an urgent time of need?"

Houston told Marshall to get going on the case, and by the end of the year, Marshall had filed a case naming the state and the university's admissions officer, S. W. Canada, as defendants in *Missouri ex rel. Gaines v. Canada*. The university and the state did their best

*Lloyd L. Gaines sought help from Marshall and the NAACP in his case against the University of Missouri.*

to tap-dance out of the accusation of racial discrimination, but after nearly two years of legal wrangling, trials, and appeals, in 1938 the U.S. Supreme Court finally ruled that the University of Missouri had to admit Gaines to its law school.

The Supreme Court victory turned hollow, however, because by the time the decision was announced, Gaines had mysteriously vanished.

Reflecting on the significance of the case decades later, Marshall said that *Gaines*

> produced the victory, the legal precedent, that we used to wipe out Jim Crow in Oklahoma, Texas, Louisiana, and other states. In *Gaines* we dragged the federal courts one more step away from "separate but equal." . . . I remember the *Gaines* case as one of our greatest victories, but I have never lost the pain of having so many people spend so much time and money on him, only to have him disappear.

Many lawyers and journalists tried to track him down, but Gaines was never heard from again. Fifty years after the case, Marshall told a reporter, "The sonofabitch just never contacted us again."

Marshall and the NAACP suffered another setback in 1938. Frustrated by the NAACP bureaucracy and weary from his around-the-clock legal work and chronic illness, Charles Houston announced that he was leaving the NAACP to go into private practice. Marshall and the NAACP couldn't convince Houston to stay, so the organization accepted his resignation and named Thurgood Marshall as Houston's replacement. His appointment as the new special counsel to the NAACP surprised no one. "Anybody who ever met Thurgood Marshall would say he was a born leader," said one lawyer. "First of all, he was just a physically imposing man. He was probably six foot three, drop-dead gorgeous, with a booming voice, a towering intellect and a fierce determination to pursue and succeed at whatever task was before him."

Under any other circumstances, Marshall's sudden rise to the top legal position in the NAACP would have been reason to celebrate, but Marshall knew, perhaps better than anyone, just how important Houston had been to the organization. "The first thing I thought about was not what it meant to me," he told one reporter, "but what a loss it was to the NAACP. No organization can afford to lose a dedicated legal giant like Charlie. Then I thought about why Houston was leaving. This man had ignored tuberculosis to give his life to the cause of freedom for Afro-Americans. I looked at his travel schedule from one end of America to the other and saw it was a killer. Buster asked me how I expected to survive such a travel schedule. I said, '. . . I'm sure I can make it till I'm forty.' She didn't think that was much of a damn joke."

With the support of the NAACP and the African American community, Marshall and his legal team continued the work that Houston had begun, but nothing could have prepared them for a trial that would deliver to Marshall one of the most devastating—and dangerous—defeats in his legal career.

On the last day of 1939, a vicious murder rocked the small farming community of Fort Towson, Oklahoma. An unidentified killer broke into the home of a white farmer, Elmer Rogers, shot him, his wife, and their four-year-old son, slashed their throats, poured kerosene over the bodies and around the house, and then set the house on fire to cover the crime. Miraculously, their nine-year-old son, Glenn, and his baby brother escaped the carnage by hiding in a closet during the attack and getting outside before the farmhouse burned down.

News of the murder screamed across the front pages of local newspapers. The grisly crime stunned Oklahomans, and soon many citizens were demanding justice—and vengeance. In response to the public pressure, police arrested two white prisoners from a local prison farm and charged them with murder. Both men confessed to the crime.

But rather than pacify the public, the arrests generated new criticism. When people learned that the two prisoners had been allowed to leave the prison, unsupervised, to visit bars and prostitutes, they were outraged. Why hadn't the state supervised its prisoners more carefully? Citizens complained that if the Oklahoma Prison System had done its job, the murders would have been prevented, and they also worried, loudly and publicly, how long it might be before other unsupervised prisoners committed crimes against Oklahoma citizens. They directed their anger and criticism toward two men: the prison warden and the governor.

Governor Leon Phillips, wanting to end the situation and its negative publicity as quickly as possible, sent one of his aides, special investigator Vernon Cheatwood, to deal with the case. A big, powerful man, Cheatwood was well known for his hard-core approach to criminal investigations and for his ability to extract confessions from almost anyone. Soon after he arrived in Fort Towson, he interviewed the convicts and ordered them released. Then, searching for a suitable scapegoat, he turned the investigation in a new, racist direction, a direction that would deflect attention from the governor and prison system.

Eleven days after the murder and only a few days into his investigation, Cheatwood ordered the local police to arrest W. D. Lyons, an African American sharecropper who had admitted to hunting rabbits near the Rogerses' farm at the time of the murders. When Lyons was picked up, he denied having anything to do with the killings.

That's when Cheatwood and his lawmen started "working" on him.

For two days Lyons lived in agony, isolation, and fear. No public defender was appointed. No phone calls were placed on his behalf. No effort was made to treat him humanely or fairly. Instead, in order to get a confession out of him, Cheatwood and his assistants deprived Lyons of food and sleep, spending the entire forty-eight hours interrogating, intimidating, and beating him. Despite the brutal torture, Lyons refused to confess.

Early in the morning of the second day, officers entered Lyons's jail cell, and the prisoner, expecting more beatings, cringed in fear. The jailers made Lyons sit up, and one of the men put a pan of charred bones on Lyons's lap, telling him that the bones had been taken from the remains of the murdered members of the Rogers family. Lyons later testified to the effect the gruesome pan of bones had on him: "They said they was the bones of Mrs. Rogers, Mr. Rogers, and the baby, and I had never seen any bones of a dead person before . . . and I was afraid of those bones on my lap in the pan. Mr. Cheatwood would lay the bones on my hands, such as teeth and body bones, and make me hold it and look at it, wouldn't let me turn my head away, and beat me on the hands and knees."

The next beating lasted at least two more hours. Lyons told Marshall that the police "beat me and beat me until I couldn't stand no more, until I gave in to them and answered the questions that they demanded." When Cheatwood again asked if he had killed Elmer Rogers, Lyons finally answered yes because, as he said, "I was forced to . . . I was beat with a blackjack, tortured all night long—because I feared I would get some more torture." Unfortunately, the battered prisoner's ordeal wasn't over yet. After he had signed a "confession," officers took him to a nearby penitentiary where they continued to threaten him. "We ought to hang and bury him right here," said one policeman. The prison warden interrogated Lyons briefly and was surprised when Lyons denied being the murderer. A deputy then took out a blackjack—a leather pouch filled with lead—and began another beating.

When Lyons couldn't take the punishment any longer, the warden called in a secretary to write up Lyons's second confession. Exhausted, bloody, and terrified, Lyons signed the confession and was taken to the basement of the prison, where guards showed him the electric chair and bragged about how many African American men had been executed in it. When the intimidation had ended, the warden had Lyons thrown in the death cell next to the electric chair to spend the rest of the night.

In early February 1940, almost a month after Lyons had been arrested, the state finally provided him with a lawyer, a white man named Stanley Belden. Belden knew that Lyons had been framed, but he also knew that he would never succeed in convincing a white judge and jury of the innocence of an African American man accused of murdering a poor white family. To complicate matters further, the Oklahoma legal system seemed content to let Lyons rot in jail. Formal charges had not been filed and no trial date had been set.

While Lyons remained locked up, a local civil-rights worker contacted the NAACP to ask for assistance, and Marshall took an immediate interest in the case. In recent years the NAACP had won a few cases where "confessions" had been beaten out of defendants. One case, *Chambers v. Florida*, wound up in the U.S. Supreme Court in 1940, and there the Court ruled that involuntary confessions cannot be used in trials. Based on the information the NAACP had received about the Lyons case, Marshall believed that the charges against Lyons should be dropped because his confession had been pounded out of him. The case provided the NAACP an opportunity to gain nationwide support by defending an African American whose treatment clearly violated the precedent established in *Chambers v. Florida*.

Marshall looked forward to the new challenge.

The Oklahoma court dawdled in prosecuting the case. Usually "justice" against African Americans was swift and harsh, but Lyons wasn't formally charged with murder until August of 1940. The judge prolonged things even more by setting the trial date for late January 1941, more than a year after the murders. The small town of Hugo, Oklahoma, would host the trial.

After a three-day train ride, Marshall arrived in Hugo and was immediately greeted by a group of African Americans who would serve as his assistants—and bodyguards—during the trial. To keep him safe from angry racists who didn't like the idea of a fancy African American lawyer coming to town, Marshall would spend each night in a different home. And a bodyguard would shadow him day and night. Though some local whites, including the father of the murdered woman, believed that Lyons was innocent, many others embraced old Jim Crow attitudes and wanted Lyons convicted and executed as soon as possible. And they didn't want an "uppity New York Negro" lawyer coming into their town to make trouble. Marshall had faced racist threats before, but the environment in Hugo pulsed with hatred, and as the focal point in a trial attended by upward of a thousand spectators each day, Marshall knew he would be an easy target. "I never wanted anyone, I mean anybody, to know that during that first night in Hugo I lay in bed sweating in fear," he told a friend. "I think I remembered every lynching story that I had read about after World War One. I could see my dead body lying in some place where they let white kids out of Sunday School to come and look at me, and rejoice."

Though he planned to do his best in the trial, Marshall had two main goals: to lay the foundation for an appeal of Lyons's conviction, and to get out of town alive.

African Americans and whites thronged to the trial to see the "Negro lawyer" take on the local white prosecutor. Through skilled questioning, Marshall tricked Cheatwood and his accomplices into admitting they had beaten Lyons, and that forced the judge to throw out Lyons's first confession. Marshall hammered away at the accusations against his client, citing over and over again the Supreme Court injunction against forced confessions and providing a string of witnesses who had seen Lyons being beaten or had heard Cheatwood and others bragging about the torture. Despite Marshall's brilliant defense, the all-white jury, under intense pressure to end the case, convicted Lyons of murder. In a surprise move, however, they reduced the sentence from death to life in prison.

The local black community celebrated this as a victory, but the loss galled Marshall, and he immediately went to work on the appeal. Meanwhile, Marshall's "victory" in Oklahoma heightened his reputation as a defender of African Americans in the clutches of Jim Crow, and the NAACP received a steady flow of requests for assistance in civil-rights cases around the country.

In 1942 the Oklahoma Supreme Court upheld Lyons's conviction, and Marshall immediately appealed the case to the U.S. Supreme Court. While that appeal worked its way through the legal system, in 1943 Marshall argued a different civil-rights case, *Adams v. United States*, his first before the U.S. Supreme Court, and came away victorious. In that case Marshall defended an African American soldier accused of raping a white woman. Marshall took the case from a Louisiana federal court, which had convicted Adams, and presented it to the court of appeals. The appeals court reviewed the evidence and Marshall's new argument, and referred the case to the U.S. Supreme Court. In the Supreme Court, the U.S. solicitor general sided with Marshall on the case, and the Court overturned Adams's conviction.

With successes like these, Marshall's reputation continued to grow, and African Americans throughout the nation started calling him "Mr. Civil Rights," believing that if anyone could shut down Jim Crow, Marshall could. With so much momentum and support behind him, by the time the Lyons murder case made it to the nation's highest court in 1944, Marshall felt confident that the justices would overturn the Oklahoma rulings and set W. D. Lyons free.

But the U.S. Supreme Court dealt Marshall a devastating, blind-side blow. In a six-to-three decision, the justices upheld the Oklahoma convictions. Lyons's second confession, they said, was legally valid because the effects of the initial beatings had worn off before he signed it.

The Court's logic confused Marshall, infuriated him, and hurt him. The faith he had in the Constitution, a faith instilled by Charles Houston and reinforced by his earlier successes in court, wavered.

Maybe, he worried, just maybe Jim Crow was invincible.

# NINE

## *Laying It on the Line*

**THE *LYONS* CASE** didn't torpedo Thurgood Marshall's legal future—he would eventually argue thirty-two cases before the Supreme Court and win twenty-nine of them—but it was one of the most painful losses of his career. Fortunately he refused to let the defeat slow him down. The NAACP had a long list of trials to prepare for, and Marshall had little time to agonize over *Lyons*. In 1944, the same year that the Supreme Court handed Marshall one of his greatest legal disappointments, he won *Smith v. Allright*, a case that, along with two others a few years later, effectively ended the racist practice of whites-only primary elections in Texas, Georgia, and South Carolina. Forty-six years later, Marshall was asked what he considered to be the biggest factor in changing race relations in

America. "The vote," he said, referring to these cases. "I think most of the change came as a result of the vote." He explained, "Without the ballot you've got no goddamned citizenship, no status, no power in this country."

More success would follow. In 1946 Marshall and the NAACP got the Supreme Court to rule in their favor in *Morgan v. Virginia*, a case that challenged racially segregated seating on interstate buses. Two years later, in *Shelley v. Kraemer*, Marshall convinced the Court to outlaw real-estate practices called "restrictive covenants" that had been used to ban the sale of homes in white neighborhoods to African Americans and other minorities. Civil-rights activists around the country hailed the triumphs as monumental progress against racial discrimination and segregation.

These legal victories encouraged Marshall and the NAACP to look for more opportunities to attack Jim Crow wherever they could find it, but Charles Houston and others had argued that an all-out legal assault on racism would be costly and time-consuming and might weaken the NAACP's efforts. As chief counsel, Marshall followed his mentor's advice and singled out public education as his organization's primary target. The sharper focus worked, and in 1950 Marshall won two Supreme Court cases against state universities (cases remarkably similar to *Murray v. Pearson*), gaining admission and equal treatment for African Americans in graduate schools at the University of Texas and the University of Oklahoma.

The Texas case revealed, once again, that the work ethic inspired by Charles Houston made Marshall a formidable opponent. The trial also showcased Marshall's courtroom skills while at the same time exposing rarely seen sensitivity. At one point he had to cross-examine a white librarian from the university's law school. As she took the stand for questioning, the woman quivered nervously, her eyes brimming with tears, and when Marshall started asking questions, she became even more upset. Her emotional reaction stumped Marshall and forced him to change from his typical hard-charging tactics to a gentler approach. He had little experience dealing with witnesses who weren't racist, mean, or dishonest. "That poor woman like to tore her handkerchief to shreds on the stand," he said after the case. "She was a good woman and you could tell she didn't want to lie. Give me the mean ones that want to lie—then I romp."

Marshall's celebrated successes against Jim Crow became a double-edged sword. African Americans and other oppressed minorities clamored for him to speak at fund-raisers, conventions, and civil-rights events. An unprecedented number of requests for advice and assistance poured into the NAACP headquarters, creating a backbreaking workload for Marshall and his lawyers. But all the acclaim also turned Marshall into a target of angry racists who saw their way of life—their Jim Crow way of life—eroding because of the NAACP's legal attacks. Marshall was constantly at risk, never more so than when he ventured into Southern states to challenge Jim Crow in court.

The NAACP caseload wearied Marshall, but he also carried a personal burden that added to his fatigue. He and Buster had always planned to have a family, but she had suffered a series of miscarriages that weakened her and dashed the couple's hopes for children. In the early 1950s her health deteriorated, and repeated visits to doctors offered no answers for her chronic illness. Her poor health and Marshall's ever-increasing professional responsibilities strained their marriage.

Concern for her husband's safety added to Buster's stress. She knew the risks he faced whenever he walked in public, and she also knew that every time he stood in a Southern courtroom, he was only one bullet away from death. Though lynchings had declined in recent years, violence against African Americans, especially those considered rabble-rousers by hostile racists, still took place. In 1951 Harry and Harriet Moore, two NAACP officials in Florida, were murdered; other prominent NAACP officials, including Marshall, regularly received anonymous threats. While he did share his wife's concerns for his safety, Marshall realized that he could not allow such concerns to keep him from his important civil-rights work. When asked if he worried about being murdered by an angry mob, he replied, "If it happens, it happens."

But his fatalistic attitude didn't prevent him from taking commonsense precautions when traveling in the South. "I'm a Southerner," he told a *New Yorker* reporter.

Born and brought up down there. I know my way around. I ride in the for-colored-only cabs and in the back end of streetcars—quiet as a mouse. I eat in Negro cafés and don't use white washrooms. I don't challenge the customs personally, because I figure I'm down South representing a client—the N.A.A.C.P.—and not myself. So up until about six months ago I had no qualms when I started out on one of these trips. . . . But I got 'em nowadays. Those boys are playing for keeps. My wife followed me out to the elevator when I left today, begging me to be careful.

His wife had good reason to be worried. In November 1946, after successfully defending two African American men in Columbia, Tennessee, Marshall and a local black lawyer named Alexander Looby got into a car to drive to Nashville. They soon realized that they were being followed by caravan of cars—a Tennessee Highway Patrol car, a squad car from the Columbia Police, and one or two more, filled with angry white men—a mob Marshall said was "com-

*Signs like this one were common in the South during the Jim Crow era.*

posed equally of state troopers and city police." After following them for a few miles, the police stopped Marshall and Looby and searched the car. Finding nothing, the officers allowed the car to continue its journey—with the caravan following close behind. About a mile down the road, the police ordered Marshall to pull over again. After questioning Marshall and Looby about who had been driving the car, a member of the mob yelled out, "That's the one! The tall yaller nigger!" Several men grabbed Marshall and put him in the backseat of the squad car and told Looby to drive off in the opposite direction. The squad car then drove down to the river, and as they approached the riverbank, Marshall saw a mob of angry white men waiting for him, and he thought that his luck had finally run out.

That very well could have been the end for Marshall, but despite the orders to drive away, Looby had followed the group down to the river, and when the mob saw him, they realized they wouldn't be able to kill Marshall without being witnessed. With their murderous opportunity lost, the local deputy driving Marshall turned his car around and headed back to Columbia. Undaunted by threats from the mob, Looby followed the squad car into town. The car stopped in front of the courthouse in the town square, and with policemen on both sides of him, Marshall went inside to meet the judge. "What's this guy charged with?" asked the judge.

As Marshall related the story later, one of the policeman replied, "Drunken driving."

The magistrate turned to me and said, "Look, I'm a teetotaler. I've never had a drink in my life. If you're willing to take my test, I'll decide your guilt or innocence."

"What's your test?" I asked.

"Blow your breath in my face," he said. So I blew my breath, and the magistrate rocked back a little bit and looked at the cop and said, "You're crazy. This man hasn't even had a drink. He's certainly not drunk."

The police reluctantly turned Marshall loose.

Shaken—and more cautious now—Looby and Marshall split up and went on to Nashville in separate cars. Marshall later heard that the mob, hungry for violence, had singled out an African American resident of the town and "beat him bad enough that he had to stay in the hospital for a month." The harrowing experience in Tennessee made Marshall much more careful on future trips, but he refused to allow the threat of violence to deter him from his mission to destroy Jim Crow. "I can testify there's times when you're scared to death," he told *Collier's* magazine. "But you can't admit it; you just have to lie like hell to yourself. Otherwise, you'll start looking under the bed at night."

The threat of violence shadowed Marshall throughout his NAACP career. On a trip to Dallas, he learned that the chief of police had warned his officers that "a nigger lawyer named Marshall was coming from New York City to cause trouble in the town" and promised that he would personally take care of the Northern rabble-rouser. After hearing about the threat, the governor ordered the Texas State Police to provide a bodyguard for Marshall while he was in Dallas—and it was a good thing he did. After a meeting in the state capitol, Marshall ran into the racist police chief. "And when he saw me," Marshall said, "he said, 'Hi, you black son of a bitch. I've got you.' And I ran. The state trooper pulled out his gun and said to the chief, 'You stay right there.'"

Marshall learned that he was not only a target of lynch mobs and state officials, but also of common citizens. Once while waiting for a train in a small Mississippi town, Marshall was confronted by a hostile stranger. "I was out there on the platform, trying to look small, when this cold-eyed man with a gun on his hip comes up. 'Nigguh,' he said, 'I thought you ought to know the sun ain't nevuh set on a live nigguh in this town.' So I wrapped my constitutional rights in Cellophane, tucked 'em in my hip pocket, and got out of sight. And, believe me, I caught the next train out of there."

When asked about his personal philosophy, Marshall once said, "I intend to wear life like a very loose garment, and never worry about nothin'," and his sense of humor about the hazards of working for the NAACP sometimes made it appear as if he really didn't worry about "nothin'." Before a trip to Louisiana, he read that an anti-integration leader there had offered a $10,000 reward for whoever killed that "burr-headed nigger lawyer from New York." When Marshall arrived in Louisiana, reporters asked what he thought about the murder contract, and he replied, "Hell, I'm not burr-headed."

Another account of Marshall's humor in the face of danger came from Ted Poston, a reporter for the *New York Post*. Poston accompanied Marshall on a trip to upstate New York to investigate police brutality against African Americans. Soon after they arrived, Marshall and Poston heard that a lynch mob was searching the area for Marshall. "I was riding with Marshall," said Poston, "and it didn't faze him in the slightest. Three times that caravan of cars passed by houses we were in. I wanted to get away from there, fast. But all that guy did was make more outlandish jokes about what that mob would do if it caught us. Not that he was foolhardy. Once he got statements from witnesses, he drove out of there without honoring the speed laws."

Marshall typically brushed aside any praise he received for his courage in the face of constant danger. The real heroes, he said, were the local activists who took on Jim Crow in their hometowns. "I don't deserve the credit. The people who dared to stand up, to file lawsuits, were beaten and sometimes murdered after I spoke my piece and took the fastest goddamn train I could find out of the area." The NAACP leaders in the South drew his special praise. "There isn't a threat known to men that they do not receive. They're never out from under pressure. I don't think I could take it for a week. The possibility of violent death for them and their families is something they've learned to live with like a man learns to sleep with a sore arm." Marshall drew strength from these examples and from earlier activists, including Frederick Douglass, of whom he said, "I don't know a Negro today, or later than Douglass, who had the courage he had." Marshall's own bravery inspired many more to stand up and speak out against racism, creating more support, more momentum for the NAACP's battle against segregation.

Not wanting to let that momentum wane, Marshall doubled his work pace, joking to one reporter, "Isn't it nice that no one cares which 23 hours of the day I work?" He traveled more than ever before, arguing cases, raising money for the NAACP's Legal Defense Fund, and rallying local support to oppose Jim Crow. One NAACP leader marveled at Marshall's ability to work so hard. "He's making a damn fool of himself, the way he works," said Arthur Spingarn. "He argues five times as many cases as the ordinary lawyer. He got off a plane from Kansas City at 3:00 a.m. yesterday; at 6:30 a.m. he was on a train headed for New Hampshire. When you urge him to slow down, you always get the same answer, 'Man, there's a job to get done.'"

The fight for civil rights couldn't rest, and neither could Marshall. One night a young lawyer named Roger Wilkins visited his apartment for dinner. "When we arrived," Wilkins said,

[his wife] told me that Thurgood wanted me in the den, urgently. He had just found out that one of the lawyers in the office had filed a defective appeal to the Supreme Court. An immediate after-hours remedy had to be fashioned, or the appeal would be dismissed.

Thurgood had initiated a series of nonstop phone calls to opposing lawyers, a justice, and court clerks. He motioned for me to crawl around through the clutter of books scattered all over the floor and research the problem while he stalled for time using his wit, wisdom, and humor. It took more than three hours of his talking and my researching, but he inhaled the law I found, made the points superbly, and perfected the appeal. Then, around midnight, we went in and had dinner with our wives.

The late nights of work, the thousands of miles on the road, and the meticulous strategizing won more cases and increased Marshall's confidence that a break—a huge break—dangled just beyond his reach. After decades of battling racism, he could sense tremors in Jim Crow's foundation, and he believed that one big case, the *right* big case, might be enough to deal a death blow to racial segregation.

# TEN

## *Taking Down Jim Crow*

**THURGOOD MARSHALL WORE** his "Mr. Civil Rights" label like a loose garment. Though his work as the point man in the NAACP's Legal Defense Fund had helped make significant dents in Jim Crow's armor, he refused to take all the credit. He didn't see himself as the mastermind behind the effort to end segregation and racism; instead, he considered himself an experienced lawyer who helped local NAACP organizations assess a situation and consider their options "because they're the ones that are gonna have to live with any action that's taken. Then I'll try to figure out how to help them do it."

Marshall told a reporter from *The New Yorker* a story that illustrated his view of himself as a leader in the Civil Rights Movement. A crowd of people sprinted down a street, trailed by a lone man, desperately trying to keep up. A curious observer stopped the man and asked, "What's goin' on here?" Marshall finished the story: "The other guy pulled loose and cried, 'Don't hold me back, man! Don't you know I'm the leader of that crowd? And if I don't run like hell they'll get away from me altogether.'" Marshall laughed and told the reporter, "That's me . . . the leader at the tail end."

Marshall knew better than anyone that he didn't work alone. As the NAACP's chief counsel, he had assembled a team of lawyers and other specialists who collaborated on specific court cases and general legal strategy. After being praised for his accomplishments, Marshall responded with self-deprecating humor: "I wouldn't want anyone to find out—but the only reason I ever look good is just 'cause I get expert advice, then follow it."

But it wasn't just the expert advice he got from his team at the NAACP that kept Thurgood Marshall looking good in court; he had other resources to sustain him through his long fight with racism: his wife and family, the training he received from Charles Houston, his commitment to civil rights, and his unshakable faith in the Constitution of the United States, especially in the Fourteenth Amendment, which granted the rights of citizenship to "all persons born or naturalized in the United States" and guaranteed all American citizens "the equal protection of the laws." From his days at Howard University, Marshall had learned that the Fourteenth Amendment would be the best way to combat racial segregation. If a court could be shown that school conditions for African Americans were *not* equal, the court would be forced to rule that the inequality violated the Constitution of the United States.

Strangely enough, not everyone believed that the Constitution could be used to win equal rights. Before the Civil War, many African Americans considered the Constitution a racist document, a set of laws that, instead of guaranteeing freedom for all citizens, shackled African Americans in the service of whites. Even Frederick Douglass, one of Marshall's heroes, had argued that slaves would never be able to use the Constitution as a weapon in their fight for freedom. In 1851, however, he had a change of heart; he had "arrived at the firm conviction that the Constitution . . . might be made consistent with its details with the noble purposes avowed in its preamble; and that hereafter we should . . . demand that it be wielded in behalf of emancipation."

A century after Douglass's declaration, Thurgood Marshall tightened his grip on the Constitution, preparing to wield it to destroy racially segregated education.

Marshall, Charles Houston, and other NAACP officials had plenty of evidence that Negro schools were terribly inferior to white schools. In many districts, black schools received less than half the funding of white schools, and the poor financial support showed up in various ways. In most states, African American teachers were paid significantly less than white teachers; in some cases, white janitors earned more than black teachers. While many white schools in the 1950s were large and modern, many black schools were single-room wooden shacks. In most rural areas, white students rode buses to school; black students had to walk to theirs. White schools had modern heating and plumbing. Black schools had coal stoves and outhouses. Where they could afford it, white schools provided up-to-date textbooks and materials and sent

A classroom in a black school in Greene County, Georgia, in 1941.

their worn-out supplies to be used in the black schools. African American students suffered under these conditions, and many dropped out of school as soon as they could find work.

Marshall built his assault on school segregation on the foundation laid by earlier legal precedents. One was established in 1908 by Louis D. Brandeis, a future Supreme Court justice. In the Supreme Court's *Muller v. Oregon*, Brandeis used medical and sociological evidence instead of legal precedents to argue that it was unhealthy for women to be required to work longer than ten hours per day. Brandeis won that case, and it was the first Supreme Court case to rely on information other than legal precedents. Marshall would follow Brandeis's lead by using sociological evidence, and would also rely on legal precedents from Supreme Court cases already won by the NAACP, cases that had whittled away at the trunk of Jim Crow.

Although he was "Mr. Civil Rights," Marshall didn't have universal support from the NAACP to rely on the Fourteenth Amendment and sociological and psychological evidence to attack school segregation. Rather than insist on racially integrated schools, some leaders in the organization wanted to use *Plessy v. Ferguson*'s separate-but-equal mandate as a way of forcing states to fund truly equal schools and colleges for African Americans. Though everyone knew it was a lie, Southern states claimed that their black schools *were* equal to white schools; under *Plessy v. Ferguson*, they argued, there was nothing wrong with having racially segregated schools. Marshall's opponents in the NAACP assumed that a court order requiring *true* equality in education would require local governments to risk bankruptcy by duplicating every educational institution and making dramatic improvements in the ramshackle black schools. The threat of bankruptcy would be enough to make white schools integrate.

After nearly two decades of battling segregation, however, Marshall felt inclined to adopt a strategy recommended by the 1931 Margold Report, a study that had been commissioned by the NAACP. In that report Harvard researcher Nathan Margold had suggested that rather than suing for true equality in education, the NAACP should mount a direct attack on the constitutional legality of racially segregated schools. Because black schools were not equal to white schools, it could be argued that inferior racially segregated schools proved that African Americans had been denied the equal protection of the laws in public education.

Marshall began laying the groundwork for that direct attack early. In a speech in 1942 he cited the previous legal successes against Jim Crow—the NAACP had won thirty of the thirty-three Supreme Court cases it had argued since 1915—and urged African Americans to demand the equal protections promised by the Constitution. He reminded his audience that existing laws had in some states already "been used

to equalize teachers' salaries and to obtain bus transportation for Negro school children. It can be used to
attack every form of discrimination against Negroes by
public school systems."

In a 1951 article reviewing the Supreme Court's
rulings on unconstitutional discrimination, Marshall
emphasized again the importance of the Fourteenth
Amendment:

> Although almost a century has elapsed since
> the Civil War and the abolition of slavery as
> an American institution, the transition of the
> Negro from a slave-chattel to a full-fledged
> free American citizen has been painfully re-
> tarded. The Fourteenth Amendment was ad-
> opted to assure that this change from slave
> status to citizenship would take place, and, in
> fact, to protect all persons against discrimina-
> tion based on race, religion, color, blood, or
> national origin.

America, Marshall reasoned, had to be sued to
enforce its own Constitution, and he believed that if

the NAACP put enough legal pressure on Jim Crow, racist institutions would collapse. Court-ordered integration would be extremely unpopular in the South, but Marshall felt it would work because "even in the most prejudiced communities, I think the majority of people have some respect for truth and some sense of justice, no matter how deeply hidden it is at times."

Of course, Marshall knew that racial equality wouldn't come without a fight, and he was prepared for it. "Mama taught me a lot," he said, "and I remember how she used to say, 'Boy, you may be tall but if you get mean I can always reach you with a chair.' Well, there's a lot of tall, mean people still around but the Fourteenth Amendment to the Constitution of the United States is a mighty big chair and I figure I can still reach a lot of 'em."

As he prepared for the most important court battle of his career, Thurgood Marshall grabbed that "chair" with both hands, ready to take on Jim Crow.

# ELEVEN

## *The Case of the Century*

**THURGOOD MARSHALL HAD** taken his first step onto the civil-rights battleground when he and Charles Houston sued the University of Maryland for refusing to admit Donald Murray to its law school. The rejection came at an opportune time for Houston and Marshall because Murray's case provided them with the legal opening they'd been waiting for: a chance to test the "separate but equal" doctrine in a court of law. They won the case and its appeal, and the victory inspired Marshall to rededicate himself to using constitutional law to fight for the rights of African Americans.

At Howard University School of Law, Houston had trained Marshall and a cadre of first-class African American lawyers to use the Fourteenth Amendment as the sledgehammer that would shatter Jim Crow someday. Their legal research convinced Marshall and his NAACP colleagues that education was the Achilles' heel of segregation law, and in the years after *Murray v. Maryland*, Marshall accepted civil-rights cases that honed his legal skills, and now he used those skills to wage battle against the laws that condemned African American children to overcrowded, underfunded, substandard schools. Marshall's place on the firing line in trials in Oklahoma, Mississippi, Texas, and Alabama gave him invaluable experience in dealing with a racist legal system and prepared him for what would become the most important civil-rights case in American history.

Of course, he wasn't working alone. While Thurgood Marshall served in the trenches of civil-rights law, the NAACP was on the lookout for a segregation case that would give them the opportunity to drive a stake through the heart of Jim Crow.

That test case finally presented itself in 1950. With the NAACP's support, Harry Briggs and other black residents in a poor county in South Carolina sued the superintendent of schools because the black schools were grossly inferior to white schools. Marshall and his team accepted the case, *Briggs v. Elliott*, knowing that they would probably lose it, but they hoped that it might end up on appeal in the U.S. Supreme Court. In the next two years the NAACP found similar school segregation cases that eventually joined *Briggs* in the appeal pipeline to the nation's highest court: *Brown v. Board of Education of Topeka* in Kansas, *Davis v. County School Board of Prince Edward County* in Virginia in 1951, and *Belton v. Gebhart* in Delaware in 1952.

In each of the trials, local courts ruled against the plaintiffs and the NAACP, but the losses didn't discourage Marshall because the NAACP had planned to assemble a foundation of school segregation cases that could be bundled and presented to the U.S. Supreme Court. Marshall and his colleagues hoped that in the country's highest court, the NAACP would be able to argue successfully that segregated schooling violated the equal protection provision of the Constitution because it inflicted educational *and* emotional damage on African American students.

For four years Marshall and his NAACP colleagues worked overtime in courtrooms, law libraries, and practice sessions. When the Supreme Court finally agreed to hear all the cases as one, officially labeled *Oliver Brown v. Board of Education of Topeka*, Marshall and his fellow lawyers celebrated.

But only briefly.

They knew that their greatest challenge lay ahead of them. They now had to prepare to meet the giant of racism in battle once again in America's grandest legal battlefield in Washington, D.C.

Segregationists called on their biggest gun to defend their racist way of life. When *Brown v. Board of Education* made it to the United States Supreme Court in December 1952, John W. Davis accepted South Carolina's invitation to defend racially segregated schooling. Davis, seventy-nine years old at the time, came out of retirement for the case, and as a former U.S. solicitor general, he would be a formidable opponent. The silver-haired Southern gentleman, the same superlawyer Marshall used to skip classes to observe, had argued more cases—140—before the Supreme Court than anyone alive.

Thurgood Marshall had argued only fifteen.

The highly political nature of the case catapulted it into the national spotlight, and naysayers on both

*Marshall with John W. Davis, his esteemed opponent in the* Brown v. Board of Education *Supreme Court case.*

sides of the racial divide predicted trouble. They worried that taking a case like this to the Supreme Court during such a volatile time in race relations might spark a violent backlash against African Americans and severely disrupt black and white schools across the nation. The tension over school segregation had already led to the murder of at least two NAACP workers in Florida, and African American activists in the South endured constant threats of violence from the

Ku Klux Klan and other racist groups. Weary of racial abuse, some African Americans were ready to fight back, even though Marshall himself warned that black violence would hurt them and their cause more than it would help. Using similar logic, some racists warned that a Supreme Court order to integrate schools would only escalate violence against blacks. Maintaining segregation, they argued, was the only way to protect African Americans from a violent white retaliation.

But no one could be sure what the Court would decide, let alone what the reaction to the decision might be. Before hearings even began, the media speculated about the possible outcomes, and most court observers considered the case too close to call. Marshall was a bright lawyer, but Davis was the grand master. The NAACP had won many civil-rights cases, but racism had a centuries-old stranglehold on Southern culture. No one, not even Marshall, knew what the nine judges would decide, but everyone agreed that they were in a highly public and incredibly awkward position. When asked about the case, one federal judge said, "It's going to be very hard for the Supreme Court to side-step the issue. And it's going to be equally hard for them to face it, with the present-day political situation what it is. The case sort of puts them on the spot, and Thurgood has maneuvered that very cleverly."

On one point, everyone agreed: the decision, whatever it turned out to be, would *not* be unanimous.

Marshall and his NAACP team spent more than a year preparing for their moment before the nation's highest court, scouring law books, interviewing people, and considering every possible legal angle. Their exhaustive preparation came straight out of the Howard University tradition. Marshall recalled,

> [Charles Houston] told us at the beginning, "Get your law and get it straight. Get your research and dig deeper. When you plan, plan twice. When you map out your case, take not the two possibilities, but assume two others. You've got to do better than the other man. Nothing can we get from the executive side of the government, nothing can we get from the legislative side. If we're going to get our rights, we're going to get it when the court moves. The court can't do it all, but the court can move

it on. Without court action in the meantime, we're dead pigeons."

Marshall drove his team hard because he felt in his bones that *Brown v. Board* was the best opportunity to force the Court—and the nation—to take action. If he failed, they'd all be "dead pigeons."

Rather than using a traditional legal attack, the NAACP team decided to argue their case based on psychological tests conducted by Dr. Kenneth Clark. It was a risky strategy, but Marshall and his colleagues figured that if these tests showed that segregation harmed African American children, the Court would be forced to apply the Fourteenth Amendment's equal protection principle to public education.

Dr. Clark's tests had presented black and white dolls to a range of African American children and asked them to identify which doll was good, which was bad; which doll they liked, which doll they disliked.

The children nearly always selected the white dolls as the good ones.

Those results gave Marshall the ammunition he

needed. "When these tests were made," he said, "to me they proved what I knew all along that the average Negro had this complex that was built in as a result solely of segregation."

In court, Marshall felt the overwhelming burden of his work, but he also felt lifted by the heritage of his mentor, Charles Houston. He recalled the scene:

> When *Brown v. Board of Education* was being argued in the Supreme Court, the entire courtroom was allotted and assigned out—every seat taken. There were some two dozen lawyers on the side of the Negroes fighting for their schools. Some of us looked around, and of those thirty lawyers, at least, we very carefully went from one to another and there were only two who hadn't been touched by Charlie Houston.

When the nine justices walked through the thick red curtains at the back of the room and took their seats behind the long mahogany bench, the three-hundred-seat courtroom crackled with tension. The moment Marshall and millions of African Americans had been waiting for, hoping for, dreaming of, had finally arrived.

When Marshall had his turn in front of the judges, he made clear the NAACP's opinion: "We are saying that there is a denial of equal protection of the law." He carefully laid out Dr. Clark's research that showed that segregation in general—not just segregated schools—hurt African American children by damaging their self-respect. He pointed out that his opponents hadn't disputed Dr. Clark's scientific evidence, and that evidence made it clear that segregation and inferior schools inflicted "not theoretical injury" but "actual injury" on African American children.

Davis countered by claiming that not only was segregation constitutional, it was *good* for African Americans. Race relations were too volatile, too complicated to allow African Americans and whites to mix in school.

The judges listened carefully, sometimes interrupting the lawyers to pepper them with questions. Marshall and Davis responded by citing legal precedents and clarifying evidence that favored their own arguments. At one point Justice Felix Frankfurter asked

Marshall to explain what he meant by "equality." Marshall replied without hesitation, "Equal means getting the same thing, at the same time and in the same place."

Throughout the hearings Marshall felt stressed and irritable, but he maintained his typical composure and professional politeness before the judges. The closest he got to letting his emotions flare came in a retort to one of Davis's arguments for the "benefits" of racial segregation. With his anger barely concealed, Marshall said,

I got the feeling on hearing the discussion yesterday that when you put a white child in a school with a whole lot of colored children, the child would fall apart or something. Everybody knows that is not true. Those same kids in Virginia and South Carolina—and I have seen them do it—they play in the streets together, they play on their farms together, they go down the road together, they separate to go to school, they come out of school and play ball together. They have to be separated in school. . . . Why, of all the multitudinous

groups of people in this country [do] you have
to single out the Negroes and give them this
separate treatment?

Marshall's argument didn't faze Davis, who continued to rely on Southern tradition and long-held racist
attitudes to make his case: "This court has spoken in
the most clear and unmistakable terms to the effect
that segregation is not unlawful. It is a little late, after this question has been presumed to be settled for
ninety years, it is a little late to argue that the question
is still at large."

In his closing argument, Thurgood Marshall reminded the justices of the earlier Supreme Court
decisions that had overturned racist policies in university education, voting, and housing, and emphasized
again the damage that racism inflicted on African
American schoolchildren:

You can have them voting together, you can
have them not restricted because of law in the
houses they live in. You can have them going to
the same state university and the same college;

but if they go to elementary and high school, the world will fall apart? And we submit the only way to arrive at that decision is to find that for some reason Negroes are inferior to all other human beings. The only thing it can be is an inherent determination that the people who were formerly in slavery, regardless of anything else, shall be kept as near that stage as is possible; and now is the time, we submit, that this Court should make it clear that that is not what our Constitution stands for.

After the hearings, the Court recessed to mull over its decision. No one knew for certain, but an announcement could come as early as the Court's next term. Five months later, word leaked to the press that the justices had indeed come to a decision.

At noon on Monday, May 17, 1954, Marshall and his team sat in the formal chambers of the Supreme Court facing the nine judges who were about to issue their decision in *Oliver Brown v. Board of Education of Topeka*. The Court reconvened by formally granting 118 lawyers admission to the Supreme Court bar, then Justice Tom C. Clark and Justice William O. Douglas each read a short decision. When they concluded at 12:52 p.m., Chief Justice Earl Warren said, "I have for announcement the judgment and opinion of the Court in *Oliver Brown v. Board of Education of Topeka*." The atmosphere in the room turned tense, and the spectators focused their attention on the chief justice.

In a booming voice, the chief justice read: "These cases come to us from the States of Kansas, South Carolina, Virginia, and Delaware. They are premised on different facts and different local conditions, but a common legal question justifies their consideration together in this consolidated opinion."

Marshall waited anxiously for Chief Justice Warren to conclude his opinion, and the crushing anticipation strained Marshall and his fellow lawyers. They had worked for years for this moment, but their work was over, and now they had to wait patiently and hope for the best.

"In approaching this problem," the judge continued, "we cannot turn the clock back to 1868, when the Amendment was adopted, or even to 1896, when *Plessy v. Ferguson* was written. We must consider public education in the light of its full development and its present place in American life."

After several more minutes, Marshall heard the beginnings of what he hoped would be the Court's final opinion. The chief justice took a breath and continued reading:

> We come then to the question presented: Does segregation of children in public schools solely on the basis of race, even though the physical facilities and other "tangible" factors may be equal, deprive the children of the minority group of equal educational opportunities? We believe that it does.
>
> Segregation of white and colored children in public schools has a detrimental effect upon the colored children. The impact is greater when it has the sanction of the law, for the policy of separating the races is usually interpreted as denoting the inferiority of the negro group.

Marshall knew then that they had won, but before celebrating, he had to wait for the entire opinion.

The chief justice referred to the psychological studies that formed the basis of the NAACP's argument. He said that the Court believed that racially segregated education did indeed harm African American children. "To separate them from others of similar age and qualifications solely because of their race generates a feeling of inferiority as to their status in the community that may affect their hearts and minds in a way unlikely ever to be undone."

Segregated schools had just been declared unconstitutional.

Marshall had won the biggest case of his career!

And it would only get better.

The judge went on, his voice even more dramatic, as if he also knew the significance of this announcement: "We conclude that, in the field of public education, the doctrine of 'separate but equal' has no place. Separate educational facilities are inherently unequal."

The announcement stunned the courtroom audience, delaying the inevitable reaction from the people on both sides of the case. Marshall would later say that when he heard the judge's conclusion, "I was so happy, I was numb." He became even happier when he realized that there would be no dissenting opinion because his team had convinced the justices to issue a *unanimous* verdict.

After the judges left the courtroom, a smiling Thurgood Marshall leaned over to one of his colleagues and said, "We hit the jackpot." The United States Supreme Court had just voted nine to zero against segregated education, and that victory put the stone in David's sling that would, in time, kill the Jim Crow Goliath.

In the celebration that followed, Marshall told reporters, "It is the greatest victory we ever had . . . the thing that is gratifying to me is that it was unanimous and on our side." He was confident that the ruling would be carried out throughout the nation because even Southern states would not dare to "buck the Supreme Court."

Indeed, to everyone on Marshall's team, it did seem like a great victory—and it was—but Marshall and the rest of the country would soon learn that the victory in *Brown v. Board of Education* was only the beginning of the fight for civil rights.

# TWELVE

*Moving to the Other Side of the Bench*

**THE GREATEST LEGAL** victory in the history of the NAACP was cause for celebration, and Marshall celebrated, of course, but he knew that his civil-rights work wasn't finished. The NAACP's monumental triumph in *Brown* knocked Jim Crow down but didn't kill it; the Court hadn't determined when integration in public schools should begin, and concerns over when that announcement would come and how it would be worded troubled Marshall.

But he was even more troubled by his wife's deteriorating health. Not wanting to worry her husband before or during the *Brown* arguments, Buster hadn't told him she had lung cancer. She died on February 11, 1955, just nine months after the conclusion of

*Marshall with his second wife, Cissy, donning the robes of a Supreme Court justice.*

her husband's most famous Supreme Court case.

To cope with the loss, Marshall returned to work with a vengeance. As a speaker and a lawyer, he was in greater demand than ever, and there was plenty of legal work to be done. *Brown* had not been the death blow Marshall had hoped it would be, and despite the Supreme Court ruling, racial discrimination, especially in Southern states, continued to plague African Americans. On May 31, 1955, the Supreme Court disappointed Marshall when, instead of declaring that school integration had to begin immediately, it created a loophole for segregationists by ordering that integration should proceed with "all deliberate speed." A reporter from *The New Yorker* asked Marshall what would happen if the NAACP won one civil-rights lawsuit after another but couldn't enforce the verdicts. Marshall replied, "That's the sixty-four-thousand-dollar question, and I'm not even going to try for it. . . . I don't know what we'd do. That's something I can't even contemplate. It would be anarchy. It would be the end of the country. I can't imagine it coming to that."

But it was coming to that. Despite all the progress Marshall and the NAACP had made, racial discrimination still prevented many African Americans from voting, from attending white schools, and from receiving fair and equal protection in the courts. But Roy Wilkins, the leader of the NAACP, refused to be discouraged. At a meeting in Atlanta he sounded optimistic when he encouraged local NAACP members to stay the course: "All these little decisions we worked out today are part of a social revolution that is taking place. The whole face of a third of America is changing—and what is achieved here in the South will also help to enhance the status of those who live outside this area and bring all of them closer to that condition we speak of so glibly in the phrase 'first-class citizenship.'"

Marshall still believed in the dream of first-class citizenship for all African Americans, but he'd been a civil-rights warrior for twenty years, and the furious legal battles had drained him. For the first time since joining the NAACP, he started thinking about a different career track. He now had a new wife—Cecilia "Cissy" Suyat, a former secretary for the NAACP—and the couple had a child on the way. It was time for him to consider slowing down and finding employment that would pay better and allow him to spend more time with his family.

But it was difficult for "Mr. Civil Rights" to unplug from the Civil Rights Movement. Shortly after returning from his honeymoon, Marshall learned that Rosa Parks had been arrested in Montgomery, Alabama, for sitting in the white section of a bus, and a young preacher named Martin Luther King Jr. had gotten involved in the boycott that followed Parks's arrest. The Montgomery Bus Boycott took off without any involvement from NAACP national headquarters, but the activists in Montgomery soon turned to Marshall for legal assistance. As a lawyer who believed in the rule of law, Marshall didn't approve of protests—violent or nonviolent—as a means of resisting racism. He told one interviewer, "I used to have a lot of fights with Martin about his theory about disobeying the law. I didn't believe in that. I thought you did have a right to disobey a law, and you also had a right to go to jail for it. He kept talking about Thoreau, and I told him, 'If I understand it, Thoreau wrote his book in jail. If you want to write a book, you go to jail and write it.'"

Despite opposing King's methods, Marshall agreed

to lend legal support to the boycott. While Montgomery protesters walked or carpooled to work, Marshall and the NAACP took the fight to court, winning a decision in Alabama that banned segregated busing. The city and state appealed to the U.S. Supreme Court, but the Court denied the appeal, and by December 1956 Montgomery's city buses were integrated.

Even though Marshall and the NAACP had done the essential legal work to integrate Montgomery public buses, King was largely credited for ending segregated busing, and for a time Marshall resented King's receiving the recognition for the NAACP's work. That resentment didn't prevent Marshall from acknowledging Martin Luther King Jr. as a great civil-rights leader, but he wouldn't admit that King was perfect in the role. "As an organizer," Marshall said, "he wasn't worth diddley-squat."

Other civil-rights cases followed, and Marshall continued working on them for the NAACP, but in 1960, he received a call to a new kind of legal work. The newly independent African nation of Kenya had begun drafting a constitution, and Marshall joined a team of lawyers who helped produce it. Already famous for his civil-rights work, Marshall's new experience in international politics earned him additional opportunities, including an appointment by President John F. Kennedy to represent the United States at several international events.

These new experiences fueled Marshall's growing restlessness with the NAACP. Times had changed, *he* had changed, and he sensed that it might be time to move on. "I thought I'd kind of outlived my usefulness," he told an interviewer, "in original ideas, in the NAACP hierarchy, what have you. And I had been shopping around, thinking of going in some law firm, making myself a good hunk of money." Marshall couldn't be certain of what might turn up, but by 1961 he was ready for something new. "I thought it was time for younger people to take over, as a matter of fact. It was a good possibility I might have gone into private practice in about five years from then. I mean, I had to look forward to taking care of a family."

Marshall would soon have the financial means to take care of his wife and two young sons, Thurgood Jr. and John, but it would come from public service, not private practice. On September 23, 1961, President

Kennedy nominated him to serve as the first African American judge on the U.S. Second Circuit Court of Appeals.

Marshall accepted the nomination as evidence of President Kennedy's commitment to the Civil Rights Movement, but his experience with the nomination process made Marshall see the president's brother—who was the United States attorney general—Robert "Bobby" Kennedy, as quite a different man. Bobby, said Marshall, "was primarily interested in getting the president re-elected . . . and was awfully ruthless. Kennedy, the president, was a very sweet man." In fact, Robert Kennedy had called Marshall to his office to insist that Marshall take a position on the trial court in New York, not on the more influential appeals court. When Marshall refused the offer, Robert Kennedy issued an ultimatum: "You don't seem to understand; it's this or nothing."

Marshall replied, "Well, I *do* understand. The trouble is that you are different from me. You don't know what it means, but all I've had in my life is nothing. It's not new to me, so good-bye." Marshall walked out of the office, leaving a shocked Kennedy behind.

Fortunately President Kennedy and Louis Martin, the vice chairman of the Democratic Party, overruled Robert Kennedy's wishes and convinced Marshall to accept the nomination to the appeals court. The nomination, however, required Senate approval, and Southern senators, still stinging from Marshall's civil-rights work, stalled his appointment for almost a year. Their efforts to block his nomination eventually failed, and on September 11, 1962, the Senate voted fifty-four to sixteen to confirm Marshall in the judgeship.

Accustomed to racist game playing, Marshall took the Southern senators' resistance in stride, and after the confirmation hearings he put a generously positive spin on their behavior: "They don't really hate me as a person, even though they barked real loud and called me everything but a child of God. They had to watch out for *their* political hides and they did whatever they had to. I'm just a symbol to them—a symbol of something that is destroying their view of the Constitution."

Marshall served only four years in the lifetime appointment before another president tapped him for public service, and this call came as a complete surprise. Marshall told an interviewer about how the new job came to be his: "I was up in the judges' dining room at the courthouse. My bailiff came up and tapped me on the shoulder. I said, 'Fred, what in the world is wrong?' I mean, he's not supposed to bother us at lunch. He was as red as a beet. I said, 'What's wrong, Fred?' He said, 'The President wants to speak to you. He's on the phone!' I said, 'The President of what?'"

President Lyndon Johnson wanted to know if Marshall would be willing to accept an appointment as solicitor general of the United States, the lawyer who represents the government in Supreme Court cases. Marshall never forgot that interview with the president.

> We chatted about it, and I said, "Well, Mr. President, I'll have to think this over." He said, "Well, go ahead, but don't tell a living soul." I said, "I assume that means nobody but my wife?" He said, "Yes, that's what I mean by nobody." He said, "Take all the time you want." . . .
>
> I went home and talked to my wife and we discussed the problems, because one was a lifetime job to trade in for a job at the beckoning

of one person. Secondly, it was a $4500 cut in salary. Third, the living expenses in Washington would be twice what I was paying in New York. So she said okay. We kept thinking about it, and the next day the phone rang. He was on the phone again. I said, "Well, Mr. President, you said I had all the time I needed." He said, "You had it." I said, "Okay."

President Johnson didn't make the announcement immediately but waited until July 13, 1965, to let the nation know that he had nominated the first African American to be solicitor general of the United States. The president told reporters, "Thurgood Marshall symbolizes what is best about our American society: the belief that human rights must be satisfied through the orderly process of law." Once again, Southern senators complained about Marshall and his qualifications, but the president had prepared well for the nomination, and the Senate confirmed the appointment on August 11, 1965.

Marshall's longtime secretary, Alice Stovall, knew that he would have to make some adjustments in his new position. "He's so informal," she said. "When he became judge we kept saying, 'We've got to make you into the image of a judge,' but with him you just couldn't do it. He would never allow his chamber doors to be closed unless he was with another judge. He would ask us, 'What have I got to be locked up about?'"

African Americans celebrated the appointment as a sign that racial equality had finally begun to take hold in the United States. President Johnson knew it would be a controversial announcement, but he was committed to placing African Americans in prominent positions as a way of showing that the government stood behind civil rights. Marshall said that President Johnson told him he made the appointment for two reasons:

> One, he thought I could handle it. Secondly, he wanted people—young people—of both races to come into the Supreme Court Room, as they all do by the hundreds and thousands, and somebody to say, "Who is that man up there with that swallow tail coat on arguing," and somebody to say, "He's the Solicitor

General of the United States." Somebody will say, "But he's a Negro!" He wanted that image, number one.

Thurgood Marshall's promotion to solicitor general created another first, one that Marshall didn't want overlooked. In a move just as sensational as his nomination of Marshall, President Johnson appointed an African American *woman*, Constance Baker Motley, to a federal judgeship. Marshall considered that hugely significant. "Everybody was saying, 'The first Negro woman!' To me that wasn't important! She was the first woman on the Second Circuit District Court. She was the first woman, not the first Negro woman—the first woman!"

In Washington, D.C., and around the country, Marshall's new job triggered optimistic speculation. If a position on the U.S. Supreme Court opened, would the president be bold enough to appoint Marshall as the first African American justice on the nation's highest court?

But Marshall would have none of it. He told reporters that the president had made it clear that the solicitor general's job was not a stepping stone to the Supreme Court; he had told Marshall, "You know this has nothing to do with any Supreme Court appointment. I want that distinctly understood. There's no quid pro here at all. You do your job. If you don't do it, you go out. If you do it, you stay here."

As solicitor general, Marshall did his job, winning fourteen of the nineteen cases he argued before the Supreme Court. That must have been good enough for President Johnson, because two years after his appointment, he dropped another bombshell.

In an oral history interview, Marshall recounted what happened on June 13, 1967. The U.S. attorney general, Ramsey Clark, visited Marshall's office one morning and made some small talk. When Marshall told him that he had an eleven o'clock appointment with some students in the White House, Clark suggested that he leave a little earlier and go to the main entrance. "The boss wants to see you."

"About what?" Marshall asked.

Clark replied, "I actually don't know."

Marshall did as requested and was ushered into President Johnson's office. After chatting for a few minutes, the president said, "You know something, Thurgood, I'm going to put you on the Supreme Court."

Marshall barely managed to respond. "Well, thank you, sir."

The two men talked for a while before going out to meet the press in the Rose Garden. With Marshall standing at his side in front of a crew of White House reporters, President Johnson read from his prepared press release:

> I have just talked to the Chief Justice and informed him that I shall send to the Senate this afternoon the nomination of Mr. Thurgood Marshall, Solicitor General, to the position of Associate Justice of the Supreme Court made vacant by the resignation of Justice Tom Clark of Texas.
>
> I believe he earned that appointment. He deserves the appointment. He is best qualified by training and by valuable service to the country. I believe it is the right thing to do, the right time to do it, the right man and the right place.

When the president began fielding questions from reporters, one asked if Marshall would explain how he felt about the new appointment. President Johnson had asked Marshall not to go into an extended news conference before he was confirmed, and Marshall, probably still in shock from the sudden turn of events, simply said, "You speak for me, Mr. President. We will wait until after the Senate acts."

When they returned from the press conference, Marshall had a request to make. "Now, Mr. President, if it's all right with you I'd like to call my wife. It would be better than for her to hear it on the radio."

Surprised, the president asked, "You mean you haven't called Cissy yet?"

"No," said Marshall, "how could I? I've been talking to you."

They got her on the phone, and after asking her to sit down, Marshall told her that the president of the United States wanted to speak to her.

President Johnson took the phone and got right to the point. "Cissy—Lyndon Johnson. . . . I've just put your husband on the Supreme Court."

"I'm sure glad I'm sitting down," Cissy Marshall said. Then she took a breath. "Mr. President, I am simply speechless. Thank you for having so much faith in my husband."

The appointment of Thurgood Marshall to the United States Supreme Court thrilled many people and, predictably, infuriated racist Southerners. Editorials in some Southern newspapers condemned the liberal president's decision and called on the Senate to block the appointment. But an editorial in the *Negro History Bulletin* suggested that President Johnson's decision would inspire many African Americans: "The rest of us must push on our way toward similar goals, each in his own small corner and in his own little way. For it has been well said by Loren Miller in *The Petitioners: The Story of the Supreme Court and the Negro* that 'as the Negro becomes a free man he becomes less and less the Court's ward and more and more his own master.'"

Marshall took his seat on the Court on October 2, 1967, joining Chief Justice Earl Warren, the judge who had presided over the *Brown v. Board* arguments, and seven other justices. The opportunity to work at this level, with these judges, reminded Marshall of his law school days when he would watch the lawyer's lawyer,

John W. Davis, and wonder if it might ever be possible for him to stand before America's most powerful
judges.

He had done that, of course, more than fifty times.
But now he had moved to the other side of the bench,
realizing an opportunity that thirty years earlier would
have been too impossible even to dream about.

# THIRTEEN

## A Minority Again

**HIS SEAT ON** the U.S. Supreme Court added to Thurgood Marshall's fame, and as a prominent legal figure, he was often called on to comment on current political events. For most of his Supreme Court career, however, Marshall declined interview requests, refused to comment on politics or politicians, and absolutely avoided making negative statements about his fellow judges. There were times, however, when he felt the need to state his views on certain topics. For example, in 1969 after violent race riots had erupted in cities across the nation, Marshall spoke out against black militants who advocated the use of violence to secure equal rights for African Americans. "I am a man of law," Marshall told an audience at Dillard University, "and in my book, anarchy is anarchy is anarchy. It

*Marshall (bottom, second from right) and his fellow Supreme Court justices prepare for their 1990 portrait.*

makes no difference who practices anarchy. It's bad, and punishable and should be punished." After clarifying that he agreed that the Civil Rights Movement still had much left to accomplish, he addressed the recent rioting in the United States:

> Nothing will be settled with a gun. Nothing will be settled with a fire bomb. And nothing will be settled with a rock. . . . It takes no courage to get in the back of a crowd and throw a

rock. Rather, it takes courage to stand up on your own two feet and look anyone straight in the eye and say, "I will not be beaten." . . . [Y]ou have to have a little faith in democracy. You see, minorities are the ones who have faith.

Move, but move within the Constitution, and find new ways of moving nonviolently within the Constitution, bearing in mind that there are many of us in this country who are not going to let it go down the drain.

Marshall's views about civil disobedience, public demonstrations, and violence were considered weak by some African Americans, including the radical leader Malcolm X. In the black community, Marshall and Malcolm X stood at polar opposites, and although the two were both famous civil-rights activists, they shared a mutual dislike for each other. Marshall told one reporter that the two men actually did meet once on Seventh Avenue in New York City. "I think we called each other sons of bitches and that was all there was." In 1977 Marshall explained to an interviewer why these two leaders disliked each other: "Malcolm X and I never got along because I just don't believe that everything that's black is right, and everything that's white is wrong." Several years later when asked about Malcolm X, Marshall showed no softening toward the black power activist: "I still see no reason to say that he is a great person, a great Negro. And I just ask a simple question: What did he ever do? Name me one concrete thing he ever did."

As a Supreme Court justice, Marshall continued to wear life like a very loose garment. His folksy stories and informalities brought a new—and to some, an uncomfortable—atmosphere to the justices' chambers. Sometimes when he'd run into the new chief justice, Warren Burger, in the hallways of the Supreme Court Building, he'd stun the stuffy, traditional chief justice by greeting him with, "What's shakin' Chiefy baby?"

Marshall's fun-loving attitude often surprised visitors to the Court building. One of his favorite stories was of the time he teased some tourists who had taken a wrong turn and ended up in the justices' exclusive elevator. Not recognizing Justice Marshall, the tourists assumed that the tall black man standing there was the elevator operator, and after one look at him, they said, "First floor, please." Marshall played along with their mistake, answering in a humble Southern tone, "Yes, massah," as the elevator headed to the first floor. When the elevator stopped, he nodded like a meek servant and held the door open for them. He loved telling the story because it illustrated not only his sense of humor but also the stereotypes that many white people imposed on African Americans.

Tourists weren't the only targets of Marshall's humor. When his clerks displeased him—or even pleased him—he'd refer to them as knuckleheads or other nicknames, and it often took new clerks some time to get used to their boss's sense of humor. Elena Kagan, nicknamed Shorty by Marshall, recalled the first time she met him. As a recent law school graduate, she had applied for a one-year appointment as one of Marshall's law clerks. He called her into his chambers, made some small talk, and then asked if she still wanted the job. Surprised by the question, she replied that she'd love to work with him, and that's when Marshall started his prank. "What's that?" he said, acting disappointed. "You already have a job?" Kagan did everything she could—yelling, shouting, screaming—to correct him, to tell him that she'd be honored to be his clerk, but to every one of her attempts, Marshall would mutter, "Well, I don't know, if you already have a job . . ." The judge finally took pity on her, Kagan said, "and assured me that I would have a job in his chambers. He asked me, as I recall, only one further question: whether I thought I would enjoy working on dissents."

In the latter part of his career, Marshall and his clerks did spend much of their time writing dissenting opinions, statements that explained the losing side's vote in Court verdicts. Marshall served as a Supreme Court justice for twenty-four years, but after the first decade of his service, the political balance shifted from liberal to conservative, and the new majority on the Court muted his effectiveness, placing him in the minority of many Supreme Court decisions and leading him to vote with the minority more than 150 times.

But before the Court turned more conservative, Marshall and his best friend and fellow liberal, William Brennan, did vote with the majority on several cases, including three that engaged the nation in lively debate: *Stanley v. Georgia* (1969), which ruled that the Constitution protected the private use of pornography;

*Furman v. Georgia* (1972), which declared the death penalty unconstitutional; and *Roe v. Wade* (1973) a decision that legalized abortion.

Marshall loved to torment his clerks by asking them paradoxical questions or by having them defend conservative legal interpretations. In these cases, he played devil's advocate, doing everything he could to stretch the young lawyers' minds. The proper definition of obscenity was a favorite topic of his, and he liked to joke about the time the Supreme Court justices and their clerks spent watching movies that were evidence in obscenity and pornography cases such as *Stanley v. Georgia*. During lunch with his clerks one afternoon, Marshall looked at his watch and exclaimed, "My God, I almost forgot! It's movie day, we have to get back." With his wry sense of humor, Marshall referred to these screenings as "a fun assignment" because during the movies he got to sit next to the nearly blind justice John Marshall Harlan and interpret what was on the screen. After some films Marshall would turn to Justice Harry A. Blackmun and quip, "Did you learn anything new from that one, Harry? I didn't."

While Marshall joked about movies at the center of the obscenity debate, he took very seriously the constitutional protection of freedom of expression. It was his belief that in the privacy of their own homes, adults could read or watch whatever they wanted. In 1969 the Court joined Marshall in a unanimous opinion in *Stanley v. Georgia* and ruled that Stanley, the plaintiff, had "the right to read or observe what he pleases—the right to satisfy his intellectual and emotional needs in the privacy of his own home." In writing the Court's majority opinion, Marshall went on to say, "If the First Amendment means anything, it means that the State has no business telling a man, sitting alone in his own house, what books he may read or what films he may watch. Our whole constitutional heritage rebels at the thought of giving government the power to control men's minds."

In an interview later, Marshall explained his stance regarding pornography. "I think grown people are entitled to do what they damn please. Ain't nobody makes you look at it. Nobody takes a gun and says you've got to. Of course it hurts children, but keep it away from them. Liquor hurts children too, keep it away from them. Drugs hurt children, keep it away from them."

Again using his interpretation of the Constitution as his foundation, one of Marshall's strongest liberal opinions regarded the death sentence. Though he had had different ideas when he was a young lawyer, as a Supreme Court justice he became convinced that the death penalty was unconstitutional. He constantly lobbied his fellow justices on the issue, and in 1972 he was able to pull out a five-to-four decision in *Furman v. Georgia*, which declared the death penalty, as imposed by according to existing state laws, unconstitutional. It may have been the majority Court decision that Marshall was most proud of. In reporting its decision, the majority wrote, "The Court holds that the imposition and carrying out of the death penalty in these cases constitute cruel and unusual punishment in violation of the Eighth and Fourteenth Amendments." In his own lengthy concurrent opinion, Marshall added in part, "We are not called upon to condone the penalized conduct; we are asked only to examine the penalty imposed on each of the petitioners and to determine whether or not it violates the Eighth Amendment." Marshall had convinced four of his colleagues that it did.

Unfortunately, Marshall's success would be short-lived. By 1976, thirty-seven states had rewritten their capital punishment laws to bring them into compliance with the *Furman v. Georgia* decision and with the Eighth and Fourteenth Amendments. After all of Marshall's efforts, the death penalty in America had been suspended for less than four years.

Marshall's advocacy for America's underclass—specifically, poor black women—was at the heart of his pro-choice support of *Roe v. Wade* in 1973. The debate over abortion brought out the worst in people—on both sides—and during the months leading up to the Court's decision, Marshall and his fellow justices received numerous death threats. The threat of violence was nothing new to Marshall, and he stuck to his principles: poor women were denied access to abortions because they couldn't afford to leave the country or pay for doctors who were able to circumvent anti-abortion laws. Women on the lower rungs of society who wanted abortions, then, suffered unfairly because they had to risk their lives at the hands of medical frauds who performed illegal abortions. Rich women, mostly white women, Marshall pointed out to his colleagues, had an unfair advantage. In Marshall's view, access to abortion should be a constitutional right. Again Marshall's lobbying helped sway some of the conservative justices to is side, yielding a seven-to-two Court decision that legalized abortion.

Throughout his tenure on the U.S. Supreme Court, Marshall gave voice to the underrepresented, reminding his colleagues on the bench that their decisions had to take into account the fact that they didn't know what it was like to be black, poor, or uneducated. But the Court that had been moderately liberal when Marshall joined it gradually changed to a much more conservative group—despite the appointment of Sandra Day O'Connor, the first female justice, in 1981. That meant that Marshall, a liberal who championed civil rights, abhorred the death penalty, and sympathized with the plight of poor and marginalized people, often had his voice drowned out by the Court's majority.

Constantly being in the minority on Supreme

Court decisions frustrated Marshall. Near the end of his career on the bench, he became more willing to vent his frustration in public. His public remarks caused a stir but also showed that Thurgood Marshall, though a minority voice on the U.S. Supreme Court, still believed in the principles he had fought for as a young NAACP attorney.

In a speech commemorating the two-hundredth anniversary of the U.S. Constitution, Marshall offended many conservatives by claiming that the Constitution was a flawed document from its beginning. The authors of the Constitution, he said, were not particularly wise or profound. Instead,

> The government they devised was defective from the start, requiring several amendments, a civil war, and momentous social transformation to attain the system of constitutional government, and its respect for the individual freedoms and human rights, that we hold as fundamental today. When contemporary Americans cite "The Constitution," they invoke a concept that is vastly different from

what the framers barely began to construct two centuries ago.

Marshall went on to point out how throughout American history, African Americans were directly affected by the Constitution and legal interpretations of the Constitution. The law, he said, made them slaves, granted them freedom, segregated them and stripped them of their right to vote, and finally granted them equal rights. "This progress has been dramatic," he said, "and it will continue." Marshall then explained how America had changed in the two centuries since the framers composed the Constitution and how the Constitution, as a living, flexible document, had been used to create conditions and opportunities that would have surprised its authors:

> The men who gathered in Philadelphia in 1787 could not have envisioned these changes. They could not have imagined, nor would they have accepted, that the document they were drafting would one day be construed by a Supreme Court to which have been appointed a woman

and the descendant of an African slave. "We the People" no longer enslave, but the credit does not belong to the framers. It belongs to those who refused to acquiesce in outdated notions of "liberty," "justice," and "equality," and who strived to better them.

Later in 1987 Marshall granted a rare TV interview, which pleased liberals and alarmed Marshall's critics, especially the former presidents that he rated according to their civil-rights records. Journalists believed that Marshall became the first modern Supreme Court justice to criticize a president currently in office when he placed Ronald Reagan at the bottom of the list. Justice Marshall also condemned Franklin D. Roosevelt and Dwight D. Eisenhower for their poor civil-rights records, singling out Eisenhower's efforts to block the *Brown v. Board of Education* decision. One president to receive Marshall's praise was, of course, Lyndon B. Johnson, the man who had appointed him to the Supreme Court. Marshall said that President Johnson's civil-rights agenda was "just unbelievable" and that Johnson's aggressive push for civil rights kept him from being reelected.

It's difficult to say what Marshall had hoped to accomplish by making these two public and provocative statements, but it is clear that both revealed his growing frustration with the conservative Court. They also reminded all Americans, if they needed reminding, that even on the Supreme Court, Thurgood Marshall hadn't changed. As he had been from his earliest days as a poor lawyer in Baltimore, Marshall remained determined to fight for the basic freedoms, the civil rights, promised by the Constitution to all Americans.

The two public statements had another result: they alienated Marshall even further from conservative politicians.

As Marshall got older, conservative groups encouraged him to retire, but Marshall remained determined to stay on the Court as long as possible. "If I die," he once told his law clerks, "prop me up and keep voting." During his career he had a few severe health problems, and almost every time he was hospitalized, rumors circulated that he was going to retire. Such speculation infuriated him, and when asked if he was considering retirement, he responded in typical Marshall fashion.

"I have a lifetime appointment and I intend to serve it. I expect to die at 110, shot by a jealous husband."

Marshall didn't live to be 110—nor was he shot by a jealous husband—but he also didn't manage to die in office. He remained on the Supreme Court until 1991, when, nearly eighty-three years old, his increasing frustration with his colleagues' conservative rulings and his own failing health finally forced him into retirement.

On June 27, 1991, he sent a letter to President George Bush, and the letter was immediately released to the press:

> My Dear Mr. President:
> The strenuous demands of Court work and its related duties required or expected of a Justice appear at this time to be incompatible with my advancing age and medical condition.
> I, therefore, retire as an Associate Justice of the Supreme Court of the United States when my successor is qualified.
> Respectfully,
> Thurgood Marshall

When Marshall broke the news of his retirement to his law clerks and saw how upset they were, he turned what might have been a sad moment into one that reminded them all of his sharp sense of humor: "When I saw *this* bunch of clerks," he said, "I shoulda quit the first week!"

At the press conference following Marshall's announcement, he showed that despite his declining health, he still possessed the old wit and biting sarcasm. Seated in a mahogany chair and surrounded by his wife, Cissy, his son Thurgood, and his law clerks and staff, Marshall fielded questions from reporters. "How do you feel?" asked one. Marshall replied with his trademark humor: "With my hands." Another reporter asked Marshall what was wrong with him, and Marshall snapped, "What's wrong with me? I'm old. I'm getting old and coming apart." Later in the press conference Marshall became especially cranky when a journalist asked if Marshall had retired because he was frustrated by being on the dissenting end of so many Court opinions.

"That's a double-barreled lie," Marshall retorted. "My doctor and my wife and I have been discussing this for the past six months or more. And we all eventually agreed, all three of us, that this was it, and this *is* it." When asked what challenges the Court might have ahead, he replied that their greatest challenge would be "to get along without me."

Marshall made few public appearances after his retirement. A lifetime of difficult, stressful work had worn out Thurgood Marshall, and just eighteen months after his retirement, Mr. Civil Rights died.

He was eighty-four.

# FOURTEEN

## *The Legacy*

**THURGOOD MARSHALL'S CAREER** helped lay the legal foundation for civil rights and also made the nation aware of the plight of African Americans. After 1954 anyone who regularly read the newspaper or watched the news knew that, despite its high-minded Declaration of Independence and Constitution, the United States did not treat all people equally.

It was a topic that even the president of the United States could not ignore.

On June 11, 1963, the day a handful of African American students—under the protection of the National Guard—integrated the University of Alabama, President John F. Kennedy appeared on television to poke the nation's racial conscience. In his elegant and measured voice, he pointed out the inequities that still existed for African Americans:

Marshall and his supporters leave a federal court hearing in Birmingham, Alabama, in 1956.

The Negro baby born in America today, regardless of the section of the Nation in which he is born, has about one-half as much chance of completing high school as a white baby born in the same place on the same day, one-third as much chance of completing college, one-third as much chance of becoming a professional man, twice as much chance of becoming unemployed, about one-seventh as much chance of earning $10,000 a year, a life expectancy which is 7 years shorter, and the prospects of earning only half as much. . . .

Then President Kennedy challenged his viewers to consider the vital importance of racial equality in America:

The heart of the question is whether all Americans are to be afforded equal rights and equal opportunities, whether we are going to treat our fellow Americans as we want to be treated. If an American, because his skin is dark, cannot eat lunch in a restaurant open to the public, if he cannot send his children to the best public school available, if he cannot vote for the public officials who will represent him, if, in short, he cannot enjoy the full and free life which all of us want, then who among us would be content to have the color of his skin changed and stand in his place? Who among us would then be content with the counsels of patience and delay?

Kennedy's speech added to the growing momentum for racial equality, and within two years Congress passed a pair of landmark civil-rights laws: the Civil Rights Act of 1964 and the Voting Rights Act of 1965. The Civil Rights Act gave teeth to the desegregation started by *Brown v. Board* by outlawing segregation in all public places. The Voting Rights Act (renewed for another twenty-five years by President George W. Bush in 2006) prohibited literacy tests and other barriers that prevented poor and uneducated minorities from voting.

Those laws helped, but still America's treatment of racial minorities lagged far behind its stated ideals. Sixteen years after President Kennedy's speech, Supreme Court justice Thurgood Marshall sounded a similar theme in an address on affirmative action:

The goal of a true democracy such as ours . . . is that any baby born in the United States, even if he is born to the blackest, most illiterate, most underprivileged Negro in Mississippi, is, merely by being born and drawing his first breath in this democracy, endowed with the exact same rights as a child born to a Rockefeller. Of course, it's not true. Of course, it never will be true. But I challenge anybody to tell me that it isn't the type of goal we should try to get to as fast as we can.

As a young lawyer, Marshall had set out to fix America's civil-rights problem, and though he made great progress, by the time he left the NAACP, he admitted, "I haven't done it yet, but I put a hole in it." He was justifiably proud of his career as a civil-rights lawyer, having had a hand in scores of precedent-setting court cases. Surprisingly, when asked to list his most important cases, Marshall put *Brown v. Board*, his most famous case, last:

The Texas primary case [*Smith v. Allright*, 1944] was the greatest. That was April 14, 1944. That, to me, was the greatest one.

A few years later, the Georgia and South Carolina primaries would be great. The Wilmington, Delaware bus case was great. The Irene

Morgan case, on bus transportation would be great. Restrictive covenants. And then the school cases.

He later confessed, "Hell, I don't know which case I'm proudest of."

But to Americans, it matters not which case Marshall was proudest of; all of his work—every investigation, every legal brief, every trial—chipped away at the foundation of racism in the United States. Thurgood Marshall is one of the twentieth century's greatest Americans not for a single act but for his long and courageous career.

His retirement in 1991 triggered a flow of tributes recognizing his outstanding service to the nation; his death in 1993 brought even more. It seemed that everyone—politicians and judges, lawyers and commentators—wanted to praise Mr. Civil Rights. His distinguished career as a lawyer, civil-rights activist, and judge spanned nearly six decades. From his earliest years as a lawyer in private practice in Baltimore to his work as solicitor general to his service on the Supreme Court, Marshall remained a dogged defender of the Constitution and human rights.

One of the most eloquent tributes came from Justice Sandra Day O'Connor, the first woman on the Supreme Court. In addition to admiring Marshall's gift for storytelling, she admired even more what he had stood for:

> Although all of us come to the Court with our own personal histories and experiences, Justice Marshall brought a special perspective. His was the eye of a lawyer who saw the deepest wounds in the social fabric and used law to heal them. His was the ear of a counselor who understood the vulnerabilities of the accused and established safeguards for their protection. His was the mouth of a man who knew the anguish of the silenced and gave them voice.

O'Connor's tribute echoed the accolades Thurgood Marshall had received throughout his career. During the *Brown* arguments one judge had said, "Marshall is unquestionably our greatest civil liberties lawyer. He's been more instrumental than any other man in professionalizing the area of law dealing with civil rights, and certainly no other lawyer and practically no member of the bench has his grasp of the doctrine of civil rights law." Two years after *Brown*, a reporter covering Marshall's work in Georgia wrote, "Few living individuals have had a greater effect than Marshall on the social fabric of America." And Marshall's nomination to the Supreme Court garnered this from *Newsweek* magazine: "In three decades, he has probably done as much to transform the life of his people as any Negro alive today, including Nobel laureate Martin Luther King."

Marshall would be the first to point out that he didn't single-handedly turn the country around, but his fingerprints are all over civil-rights history. Thanks to his efforts, African Americans and other minorities today are no longer shackled by Jim Crow. Like white Americans, they are free to live where they choose, attend schools where they choose, and vote for whom they choose. Segregated buses, restaurants, and bathrooms are a thing of the past. The law in the twenty-first century is more color-blind than it ever was, and the protections and promises of the Constitution now apply to more people than ever before.

Of course, America still struggles with racial issues. In 2007, six African American teenagers in Jena, Louisiana, were charged with attempted murder for participating in a school fight that began after white students hung nooses in a school-yard tree. In that same year, the U.S. Supreme Court issued a five-to-four decision ruling that schools in Washington and Kentucky could *not* use race as a factor in assigning students to public schools. Many felt that this decision would be the start of a movement to overturn *Brown v. Board of Education* because it nullified busing and other programs that had been designed to promote racial balance in school populations. Still, in terms of race relations, America is better than it was when Marshall first started his legal battles for equality; it's clear, however, that our nation must not forget the gains that our greatest civil-rights warrior fought for and won.

To the end of his life, Marshall maintained that the rule of law could make America a better, freer country, but on July 4, 1992, in one of his last speeches, he conceded that it was the responsibility of each citizen to take to heart the racial lessons the law taught, and

he pleaded with his audience to recognize the value of
all people:

> The legal system can force open doors, and,
> sometimes, even knock down walls. But it
> cannot build bridges. That job belongs to you
> and me. We can run from each other, but we
> cannot escape each other. We will only attain
> freedom if we learn to appreciate what is differ-
> ent and muster the courage to discover what is
> fundamentally the same. Take a chance, won't
> you? Knock down the fences that divide. Tear
> apart walls that imprison. Reach out: freedom
> lies just on the other side.

# SOURCE NOTES

**I BEGAN MY RESEARCH** on Thurgood Marshall by reading two biographies: Juan Williams's *Thurgood Marshall: American Revolutionary*, and Carl T. Rowan's *Dream Makers, Dream Breakers: The World of Justice Thurgood Marshall*. From there I went to the Internet and explored sites that covered Marshall's career in civil rights, especially the *Brown v. Board* case. I was often sidetracked into tangential information about the Civil Rights Movement and the historical foundations of slavery and racial discrimination in the United States—such meanderings are highly interesting and are occupational hazards for the historical researcher.

With a basic understanding of Marshall and his era, I next searched for primary documents: court records, photographs, and contemporaneous newspaper and magazine articles about Marshall or his career. *Thurgood Marshall: His Speeches, Writings, Arguments,*

*Opinions, and Reminiscences*, edited by Mark V. Tushnet, provided an excellent starting point for this part of my research. Michael D. Davis and Hunter R. Clark's engaging and thorough biography, *Thurgood Marshall: Warrior at the Bar, Rebel on the Bench,* provided perspectives and references that didn't appear in other sources.

For historical background I read works about important figures such as Frederick Douglass, Booker T. Washington, W. E. B. Du Bois, Louis D. Brandeis, and others; historical documents such as the Declaration of Independence, the U.S. Constitution, the Bill of Rights, and so on; and arguments by abolitionists and racists defending their stances on the slavery issue.

My research convinced me that the most compelling aspect of Marshall's career was his work from the late 1930s to 1961. His career as a judge, though important, seemed less interesting, in part because the flamboyant and outspoken Marshall was necessarily constrained by the ethics and code of conduct imposed on federal judges. Ample material, however, is available regarding his career as judge, especially as a justice on the U.S. Supreme Court.

## EPIGRAPH

"The interesting things . . .": Pierce, "The Solicitor General," 77.

## FOREWORD

"got himself killed": Evers-Williams, *For Us, the Living*, 58.

"If Whites could . . .": Williams, "The Thurgood Marshall Nobody Knows," 68.

## INTRODUCTION

"I have for . . .": Kluger, *Simple Justice*, 702; Rowan, *Dream Makers*, 216.

"These cases come . . ." and "In approaching this . . .": "Civil Rights, *Brown v. Board of Education* (1954)," online.

## CHAPTER ONE

"We hold these truths . . .": Declaration of Independence, online.

"declaring the Negro . . .": *Virtual Jamestown: Laws on Slavery*, online.

"beings of an . . ." and "We think they . . .": "Dred Scott Case," online.

"all persons born . . . of the laws": Fourteenth Amendment to the U.S. Constitution, online.

"Because one of . . .": Fenderson, *Thurgood Marshall*, 54.

"We think the . . ." and "legislation is powerless . . .": *Plessy v. Ferguson*, Mr. Justice Brown, online.

"The destinies of . . .": *Plessy v. Ferguson*, Mr. Justice Harlan, online.

## CHAPTER TWO

"and he collected . . .": Rowan, *Dream Makers*, 39.

"The high school . . .": Rowan, *Dream Makers*, 37.

"There is no . . .": Davis and Clark, *Thurgood Marshall*, 8.

"No race can . . .": Washington, *Up from Slavery*, online.

"The negro should . . .": Dickson, "The Vardaman Idea," online.

"We claim for . . .": "Niagara Movement," online.

## CHAPTER THREE

"was one of . . .": Pierce, "The Solicitor General," 67.

"This part of . . .": Pierce, "The Solicitor General," 68.

"timid little boy . . .": Pierce, "The Solicitor General," 67.

"See that he . . .": Rowan, *Dream Makers,* 35.

"he stopped crying . . .": Pierce, "The Solicitor General," 67.

"beat the stuffing . . .": Rowan, *Dream Makers*, 35.

"I didn't like . . .": Rowan, *Dream Makers*, 38; Williams, *Thurgood Marshall*, 26.

"goofing off, driving . . .": Rowan, *Dream Makers*, 33.

"was always playing . . ." and "He used to . . .": Williams, *Thurgood Marshall*, 28–29.

"you'd break yourself . . .": Williams, *Thurgood Marshall*, 29.

"We used to . . .": Tushnet, *Thurgood Marshall*, 500.

"The only relations . . .": Tushnet, *Thurgood Marshall*, 413.

"I remember very . . .": Tushnet, *Thurgood Marshall*, 413–414.

"In Baltimore, where . . .": Taper, "A Reporter at Large," 86–87; "Mr. Justice Marshall," *Newsweek*, 35.

"I heard a . . .": Taper, "A Reporter at Large," 87.

"My dad and . . .": Tushnet, *Thurgood Marshall*, 500.

"He had a . . .": Williams, *Thurgood Marshall*, 32–33.

"Your mother and . . .": Williams, *Thurgood Marshall*, 27.

"I would talk . . .": Tushnet, *Thurgood Marshall*, 417.

"From what she . . .": Tushnet, *Thurgood Marshall*, 419–20.

"they provided something . . ." and "She didn't believe . . .": Rowan, *Dream Makers*, 38.

"My mother—believe . . .": Tushnet, *Thurgood Marshall*, 417.

"The dislike between . . .": Williams, *Thurgood Marshall*, 41–42.

"Thurgood was full . . .": Williams, *Thurgood Marshall*, 35.

"take a motor . . .": Rowan, *Dream Makers*, 40.

"If you don't . . .": Rowan, *Dream Makers*, 35.

"Before I left . . .": "The Law," *Time*, 26.

"We could hear . . .": Williams, *Thurgood Marshall*, 35.

"I didn't get . . .": Tushnet, *Thurgood Marshall*, 500.

## CHAPTER FOUR

"My father, I . . .": Rowan, *Dream Makers*, 38.

"If anyone calls . . .": Pierce, "The Solicitor General," 69.

"Don't you ever . . . like that": "The Law," *Time*, 24; Rowan, *Dream Makers*, 35–36; Williams, *Thurgood Marshall*, 15–16.

"I'm really sorry . . . sure did": Rowan, *Dream Makers*, 36.

"He really came . . .": Rowan, *Dream Makers*, 34; Tushnet, *Thurgood Marshall*, 420.

"After all, . . . to hell": "The Law," *Time*, 24.

"There is little . . . enjoy as a right": Williams, *Thurgood Marshall*, 31.

"I later learned . . .": Rowan, *Dream Makers*, 37.

"My father was . . .": Rowan, *Dream Makers*, 70.

"very good ability.": Williams, *Thurgood Marshall*, 39.

## CHAPTER FIVE

"the least likely . . .": Williams, *Thurgood Marshall*, 42.

"He was suspended . . ." and "They didn't need . . .": Rowan, *Dream Makers*, 43.

"You are fired! . . ." and "I figure it's . . .": Williams, *Thurgood Marshall*, 44–45.

"had great trouble . . .": Tushnet, *Thurgood Marshall*, 414.

"At times I . . .": Rowan, *Dream Makers*, 44.

"Nigger, why don't . . ." and "We found out . . .": Davis and Clark, *Thurgood Marshall*, 44–45.

"We desegregated the . . .": Davis and Clark, *Thurgood Marshall*, 45; Hengstler, "Looking Back," 58; see also Williams, *Thurgood Marshall*, 48–49.

"at least nine . . .": Rowan, *Dream Makers*, 43.

"I just eased . . .": Tushnet, *Thurgood Marshall*, 415.

"because we learned . . .": Davis and Clark, *Thurgood Marshall*, 45.

"he was so . . .": Williams, *Thurgood Marshall*, 50.

"First . . . you look . . .": Rowan, *Dream Makers*, 38.

"We decided to . . .": Davis and Clark, *Thurgood Marshall*, 45.

"to be on . . .": Tushnet, *Thurgood Marshall*, 415.

**CHAPTER SIX**

"seems to have . . .": "Mr. Justice Marshall," *Newsweek*, 35.

"My dad, my . . .": Tushnet, *Thurgood Marshall*, 415; Williams, *Thurgood Marshall*, 38.

"Oh yes, . . . we . . .": Williams, *Thurgood Marshall*, 35.

"My father never . . .": "Mr. Justice Marshall," *Newsweek*, 35.

"dummy's retreat . . . because . . .": Williams, *Thurgood Marshall*, 53.

"You're going . . . I'll . . .": Rowan, *Dream Makers*, 46.

"I'd got the . . .": Poling, "Thurgood Marshall and the Fourteenth Amendment," 147.

"Every man here . . ." and "The only thing . . .": Tushnet, *Thurgood Marshall*, 273.

"I never worked . . .": Rowan, *Dream Makers*, 68.

"We went to . . .": Gormley, "A Mentor's Legacy," 64; see also Rowan, *Dream Makers*, 67–68.

"Any lawyer who . . .": "May It Please the Court," *Time*, 18.

"Every time John . . .": "May It Please the Court," *Time*, 19; Williams, *Thurgood Marshall*, 57.

"[what] Charlie beat . . .": Davis and Clark, *Thurgood Marshall*, 55.

"when you get . . ." "You've got to . . ." "be social engineers . . ." and "turn this whole . . .": Tushnet, *Thurgood Marshall*, 273.

## CHAPTER SEVEN

"If you want . . .": Davis and Clark, *Thurgood Marshall*, 70.

"had a genius . . .": Poling, "Thurgood Marshall and the Fourteenth Amendment," 147.

"She would bring . . .": Tushnet, *Thurgood Marshall*, 419; "Mr. Justice Marshall," *Newsweek*, 35.

"Once in a . . .": Williams, *Thurgood Marshall*, 63.

"I bought some . . .": Rowan, *Dream Makers*, 70.

"wouldn't admit Negroes. . . ." and "I said one . . .": Hengstler, "Looking Back," 61.

"wasn't a good . . .": Tushnet, *Thurgood Marshall*, 419.

"I don't have . . . you for nothing": Tushnet, *Thurgood Marshall*, 419; see also Davis and Clark, *Thurgood Marshall*: 70–71; Williams, *Thurgood Marshall*, 63; Fenderson, *Thurgood Marshall*, 77–78.

"It was all . . .": Zion, "Thurgood Marshall Takes a New 'Tush-Tush' Job," 70.

"Start paying me . . .": Williams, *Thurgood Marshall*, 74.

"My first idea . . .": Tushnet, *Thurgood Marshall*, 418.

"One day I . . .": Tushnet, *Thurgood Marshall*, 418–20; see also Gormley, "A Mentor's Legacy," 64; Williams, *Thurgood Marshall*, 77.

"What's at stake . . .": Davis and Clark, *Thurgood Marshall*, 87.

"set the colored . . .": Davis and Clark, *Thurgood Marshall*, 88.

"I worked the . . .": Davis and Clark, *Thurgood Marshall*, 90.

## CHAPTER EIGHT

"The ringleader got . . .": Williams, *Thurgood Marshall*, 66.

"I got the . . . Polo Grounds" and "I felt that . . .": Rowan, *Dream Makers*, 70.

"Charles Hamilton Houston . . .": Smith and Ellis, "Thurgood Marshall Before the Court," online.

"How very tush-tush . . . what happened": Zion, "Thurgood Marshall Takes a New 'Tush-Tush' Job," 11; see also Poling, "Thurgood Marshall and the Fourteenth Amendment," 143; Davis and Clark, *Thurgood Marshall*, 105.

"I am appealing . . .": Rowan, *Dream Makers*, 71.

"produced the victory . . ." and "The sonofabitch just . . .": Rowan, *Dream Makers*, 78.

"Anybody who ever . . .": Smith and Ellis, "Thurgood Marshall Before the Court," online.

"The first thing . . .": Rowan, *Dream Makers*, 76.

"They said they . . ." "beat me and . . ." and "I was forced . . .": Tushnet, *Thurgood Marshall*, 6.

"We ought to . . .": Tushnet, *Thurgood Marshall*, 7.

"I never wanted . . .": Rowan, *Dream Makers*, 107.

## CHAPTER NINE

"The vote . . . I . . .": "*Ebony* Interview with Supreme Court Justice Thurgood Marshall," 218.

"Without the ballot . . .": Rowan, *Dream Makers*, 129.

"That poor woman . . .": Poling, "Thurgood Marshall and the Fourteenth Amendment," 152.

"If it happens . . .": Rowan, *Dream Makers*, 113.

"I'm a Southerner . . .": Taper, "A Reporter at Large," 84.

"composed equally of . . .": Rowan, *Dream Makers*, 108.

"That's the one! . . ." "What's this guy . . . certainly not drunk" and "beat him bad . . .": Rowan, *Dream Makers*, 109.

"I can testify . . .": Poling, "Thurgood Marshall and the Fourteenth Amendment," 154.

"a nigger lawyer . . .": Davis and Clark, *Thurgood Marshall*, 106; Williams, *Thurgood Marshall*, 103–4.

"And when he . . .": Davis and Clark, *Thurgood Marshall*, 106; Williams, *Thurgood Marshall*, 104.

"I was out . . .": "The Law," *Time*, 24; see also Davis and Clark, *Thurgood Marshall*, 108; Rowan, *Dream Makers*,112–13; and Williams, *Thurgood Marshall*, 106–7.

"I intend to . . .": Poling, "Thurgood Marshall and the Fourteenth Amendment," 143.

"burr-headed nigger . . . Hell, I'm not . . .": Rowan, *Dream Makers*, 115.

"I was riding . . .": Poling, "Thurgood Marshall and the Fourteenth Amendment," 153–54.

"I don't deserve . . .": Rowan, *Dream Makers*, 112–13.

"There isn't a . . .": "Mr. Justice Marshall," *Newsweek*, 23.

"I don't know . . .": Tushnet, *Thurgood Marshall*, 420.

"Isn't it nice . . .": Zion, "Thurgood Marshall Takes a New 'Tush-Tush' Job," 11.

"He's making a . . .": Poling, "Thurgood Marshall and the Fourteenth Amendment," 155.

"When we arrived . . .": Wilkins, "Thurgood and Me," 14.

## CHAPTER TEN

"because they're the . . ." and "What's goin' on . . . the tail end": Taper, "A Reporter at Large," 88.

"I wouldn't want . . .": Poling, "Thurgood Marshall and the Fourteenth Amendment," 148.

"arrived at the . . .": Douglass, "Change of Opinion," online.

"been used to . . .": "Thurgood Marshall: The Legal Attack," online.

"Although almost a . . .": Tushnet, *Thurgood Marshall*, 116.

"even in the . . .": Poling, "Thurgood Marshall and the Fourteenth Amendment," 146.

"Mama taught me . . .": Poling, "Thurgood Marshall and the Fourteenth Amendment," 156.

## CHAPTER ELEVEN

"It's going to . . .": Poling, "Thurgood Marshall and the Fourteenth Amendment," 149.

"[Charles Houston] told . . .": Tushnet, *Thurgood Marshall*, 274.

"When these tests . . .": Tushnet, *Thurgood Marshall*, 499.

"When *Brown v. Board* . . .": Tushnet, *Thurgood Marshall*, 272; Gormley, "A Mentor's Legacy," 66.

"We are saying . . ." "not theoretical injury" and "actual injury": Williams, *Thurgood Marshall*, 216.

"Equal means getting . . .": Fenderson, *Thurgood Marshall*, 100.

"I got the . . .": "The Law," *Time*, 27.

"This court has . . .": and "You can have . . .": Smith and Ellis, "Thurgood Marshall Before the Court," online.

"I have for . . .": Kluger, *Simple Justice*, 702; Rowan, *Dream Makers*, 216.

"These cases come . . ." "In approaching this . . ." "We come then . . ." "Segregation of white . . ." "To separate them . . ."

and "We conclude that . . .": "Civil Rights, *Brown v. Board of Education* (1954)," online.

"I was so . . .": "The Law," *Time*, 27.

"We hit the . . .": Williams, *Thurgood Marshall*, 226; Rowan, *Dream Makers*, 218.

"It is the . . .": Williams, *Thurgood Marshall*, 227.

"buck the Supreme . . .": Williams, *Thurgood Marshall*, 226.

## CHAPTER TWELVE

"That's the sixty-four-thousand-dollar . . .": Taper, "A Reporter at Large," 114.

"All these little . . .": Taper, "A Reporter at Large," 124–25.

"I used to . . .": Tushnet, *Thurgood Marshall*, 471.

"As an organizer . . .": Tushnet, *Thurgood Marshall*, 472.

"I thought I'd . . .": Tushnet, *Thurgood Marshall*, 464.

"I thought it . . .": Marshall, Interview, 6.

"was primarily interested . . ." "You don't seem . . ." and "Well I do . . .": Tushnet, *Thurgood Marshall*, 484.

"They don't really . . .": Fenderson, *Thurgood Marshall*, 108–9.

"I was up . . .": Marshall, Interview, 7.

"We chatted about . . .": Marshall, Interview, 7–8.

"Thurgood Marshall symbolizes . . .": Pierce, "The Solicitor General," 68.

"He's so informal . . .": Pierce, "The Solicitor General," 74.

"One, he thought . . .": Marshall, Interview, 8.

"Everybody was saying . . .": Marshall, Interview, 12.

"You know this . . .": Marshall, Interview, 8.

"The boss wants . . . thank you, sir": Marshall, Interview, 10–11.

"I have just . . ." and "You speak for . . .": "Texts of Johnson Statement on Marshall," 18.

"Now, Mr. President . . . faith in my husband": Marshall, Interview, 11.

"The rest of . . .": "Supreme Court Justice Thurgood Marshall," 5.

## CHAPTER THIRTEEN

"I am a . . .": Marshall, "A Supreme Court," 92.

"Nothing will be . . .": Marshall, "A Supreme Court," 93.

"I think we . . .": Williams, *Thurgood Marshall*, 301.

"Malcolm X and . . .": Tushnet, *Thurgood Marshall*, 433–34.

"I still see . . .": Hengstler, "Looking Back," online.

"What's shakin' Chiefy . . .": Woodward and Armstrong, *The Brethren*, 59.

"First floor, please . . .": Kluger, *Simple Justice*, 59.

"What's that? . . . working on dissents": Kagan, "In Memoriam," 1126.

"My God, I . . .": Woodward and Armstrong, *The Brethren*, 198.

"Did you learn . . .": Rowan, *Dream Makers*, 341.

"the right to . . ." and "If the first . . .": Goldman and Gallen, *Thurgood Marshall*, 282.

"I think grown . . .": Williams, *Thurgood Marshall*, 345.

"The Court holds . . .": Goldman and Gallen, *Thurgood Marshall*, 354.

"We are not . . .": Goldman and Gallen, *Thurgood Marshall*, 355.

"The government they . . .": Marshall, "Reflections on the Bicentennial of the United States Constitution," 2.

"This progress has . . ." and "The men who . . .": Marshall, "Reflections on the Bicentennial of the United States Constitution," 5.

"just unbelievable": Williams, *Thurgood Marshall*, 383.

"If I die . . .": Lacayo, "Marshall's Legacy," 25.

"I have a . . .": Williams, "The Thurgood Marshall Nobody Knows," 74.

"My Dear Mr. . . .": "My Dear Mr. President," A13.

"When I saw . . .": Brewer, "In Memoriam," 1121.

"How do you . . . get along without me": Davis and Clark, *Thurgood Marshall*, 8.

## CHAPTER FOURTEEN

"The Negro baby . . ." and "The heart of . . .": Kennedy, "Radio and Television Report to the American People on Civil Rights," online.

"The goal of . . .": Tushnet, *Making Civil Rights Law*, 5.

"I haven't done . . .": Pierce, "The Solicitor General," 68.

"The Texas primary . . .": Tushnet, *Thurgood Marshall*, 512.

"Hell, I don't . . .": Rowan, *Dream Makers*, 129.

"Although all of . . .": *Thurgood Marshall, Associate Justice of the Supreme Court*, 213.

"Marshall is unquestionably . . .": Poling, "Thurgood Marshall and the Fourteenth Amendment," 141.

"Few living individuals . . .": Taper, "A Reporter at Large," 80.

"In three decades . . .": "Mr. Justice Marshall," *Newsweek*, 34.

"The legal system . . .": Marshall, "Liberty Medal Acceptance Speech," online.

# BIBLIOGRAPHY
## WORKS CITED

Andrews, William L., ed. *The Oxford Frederick Douglass Reader*. New York: Oxford, 1996.

Balkin, Jack M. Brown v. Board of Education Web site. www.yale.edu/lawweb/jbalkin/brown/index.html.

Balkin, Jack M. *An Interactive Civil Rights Chronology*. www.yale.edu/lawweb/jbalkin/brown/1502.html.

Bland, Randall W. *Private Pressure on Public Law: The Legal Career of Justice Thurgood Marshall: 1934–1991*, rev. ed. Lanham, MD: University Press of America, 1993.

Brewer, Scott. "In Memoriam: Justice Marshall's Justice Martial." *Texas Law Review*, May 1993, 1121–1124.

"*Brown v. Board of Education* (1954)." Landmark Cases: Supreme Court. www.landmarkcases.org/brown/marshall.html.

Brown v. Board of Education *National Historic Site*. www.nps.gov/brvb.

"Civil Rights, *Brown v. Board of Education* (1954)," Historical Documents in United States History, www.historicaldocuments.com/BrownvBoardofEducation.htm

Davis, Michael D., and Hunter R. Clark. *Thurgood Marshall: Warrior at the Bar, Rebel on the Bench.* New York: Birch Lane Press, 1992.

Declaration of Independence. http://www.archives.gov/national-archives-experience/charters/declaration.html.

Dickson, Harris. "The Vardaman Idea: How the Governor of Mississippi Would Solve the Race Question." *The Saturday Evening Post*, 27 April 1907. www.hhtc.org/vw/b11/sep-txt.html.

Douglass, Frederick. "Change of Opinion Announced." *The North Star*, May 23, 1851. www.teachingamericanhistory.org/library/index.asp?document1107.

"Dred Scott Case: The Supreme Court Decision." *Africans in America.* www.pbs.org/wgbh/aia/part4/4h2933t.html.

"*Ebony* Interview with Supreme Court Justice Thurgood Marshall." *Ebony*, November 1990, 216–22.

Evers-Williams, Myrlie. *For Us, the Living.* Jackson, Miss.: Banner Books, 1967, 1996.

Fenderson, Lewis H. *Thurgood Marshall: Fighter for Justice.* New York: McGraw Hill, 1969.

Fourteenth Amendment to the U.S. Constitution. www.nps.gov/malu/documents/amend14.htm.

Goldman, Roger, and David Gallen. *Thurgood Marshall: Justice for All*. New York: Carroll & Graf, 1992.

Gormley, Ken. "A Mentor's Legacy: Charles Hamilton Houston, Thurgood Marshall and the Civil Rights Movement." *ABA Journal* 78 (June 1, 1992), 62–66.

Hengstler, Gary A. "Looking Back: Reflections on a Life Well-Spent." *ABA Journal* 78 (June 1, 1992), 56. http://www.proquest.com.

Kagan, Elena. "In Memoriam: For Justice Marshall." *Texas Law Review*, May 1993, 1125–30.

Kennedy, John F. "Radio and Television Report to the American People on Civil Rights." June 11, 1963. www.jfklibrary.org.

Kluger, Richard. *Simple Justice: The History of* Brown v. Board of Education *and Black America's Struggle for Equality*. New York: Knopf, 1976.

Lacayo, Richard. "Marshall's Legacy: A Lawyer Who Changed America." *Time*, July 8, 1991, 24–25.

"The Law: The Tension of Change." *Time*, September 19, 1955, 23–27.

Marshall, Thurgood. Interview by T. H. Baker, July 10, 1969. Oral History Interview I, transcript. Internet copy, LBJ Library. http://www.lbjlib.utexas.edu/johnson/archives.hom/oralhistory.hom/MarshallT/marshall.pdf.

———. "Liberty Medal Acceptance Speech." July 4, 1994.

http://www.constitutioncenter.org/libertymedal/recipient_1992_speech.html.

———. "Reflections on the Bicentennial of the United States Constitution." *Harvard Law Review* 101, no. 1 (November 1987), 1–5.

———. "A Supreme Court Justice's Warning to Fellow Negroes." *U.S. News and World Report* 66, no. 20 (May 19, 1969): 92–93.

"May It Please the Court." *Time*, December 21, 1953, 18–19.

"Mr. Justice Marshall." *Newsweek*, June 26, 1967, 34–36.

"My Dear Mr. President." *New York Times*, June 28, 1991, A13.

"Niagara Movement (1905–10)." *The Rise and Fall of Jim Crow.* http://www.pbs.org/wnet/jimcrow/stories_events_niagara.html.

Pierce, Ponchitta. "The Solicitor General." *Ebony*, November 1965, 67–77.

*Plessy v. Ferguson*, 163 U.S. 537 (1896), Mr. Justice Brown. www.tourolaw.edu/patch/plessy/Brown.asp.

*Plessy v. Ferguson*, 163 U.S. 537 (1896), Mr. Justice Harlan. www.tourolaw.edu/patch/plessy/Harlan.asp.

Poling, James. "Thurgood Marshall and the Fourteenth Amendment." In *Reporting Civil Rights: Part I, American Journalism 1941–1963*, 141–56. New York: Library of America, 2003.

Rowan, Carl T. *Dream Makers, Dream Breakers: The World of Justice Thurgood Marshall.* New York: Welcome Rain, 1993.

Smith, Stephen, and Kate Ellis. "Thurgood Marshall Before the Court." *American RadioWorks.* http://americanradioworks. publicradio.org/features/marshall.

"The Supreme Court: The Fading Line." *Time*, December 21, 1953, 15–19.

*The Supreme Court Historical Society.* www.supremecourthistory.org

"Supreme Court Justice Thurgood Marshall." *Negro History Bulletin* 30, no. 6 (October 1967), 4–5.

Taper, Bernard. "A Reporter at Large: A Meeting in Atlanta." *The New Yorker*, March 17, 1956, 80–127.

"Texts of Johnson Statement on Marshall and News Conference on Various Issues," *New York Times*, June 14, 1967, 18.

*Thurgood Marshall, Associate Justice of the Supreme Court: Memorial Tributes in the Congress of the United States.* Washington, D.C.: U.S. Government Printing Office, 1994.

"Thurgood Marshall: The Legal Attack to Secure Civil Rights. Chicago, IL, July 13, 1942." www.calvin.edu/academic/cas/ programs/pauleyg/voices/marshal2.htm.

Tushnet, Mark V. *Making Civil Rights Law: Thurgood Marshall and the Supreme Court, 1936–1961.* New York: Oxford University Press, 1994.

———. *Making Constitutional Law: Thurgood Marshall and the Supreme Court, 1961–1991.* New York: Oxford University Press, 1997.

———, ed. *Thurgood Marshall: His Speeches, Writings, Arguments, Opinions, and Reminiscences.* Chicago: Lawrence Hill, 2001.

*Virtual Jamestown: Laws on Slavery.* October 1705-Chap. XXII. www.virtualjamestown.org/laws1.html.

Washington, Booker, T. *Up from Slavery: An Autobiography,* electronic ed. www.wfu.edu/%7Ezulick/341/booker.html.

Weil, Martin, and Stephanie Griffith. "Marshall Transformed Nation in the Courts." *Washington Post,* January 25, 1993, A11.

Wilkins, Roger. "Thurgood and Me." *Mother Jones,* November/December 1991, 13–14.

Williams, Juan. "Marshall's Law." *The Washington Post Magazine,* January 7, 1990, 12–16.

———. *Thurgood Marshall: American Revolutionary.* New York: Three Rivers Press, 1998.

———. "The Thurgood Marshall Nobody Knows." *Ebony,* May 1990, 68–76.

Woodward, Bob, and Scott Armstrong. *The Brethren: Inside the Supreme Court.* New York: Simon and Schuster, 1979.

Zion, Sidney E. "Thurgood Marshall Takes a New 'Tush-Tush' Job." *The New York Times Magazine,* August 22, 1965, 11, 68–71.

# FOR FURTHER READING

Bland, Randall W. *Private Pressure on Public Law: The Legal Career of Justice Thurgood Marshall: 1934–1991*, rev. ed. Lanham, MD: University Press of America, 1993.

**After a brief chapter on Marshall's life, this book turns to his legal career, from his early private practice in Baltimore to his career on the U.S. Supreme Court.**

Davis, Michael D., and Hunter R. Clark. *Thurgood Marshall: Warrior at the Bar, Rebel on the Bench*. New York: Birch Lane Press, 1992.

**An engaging biography, one that devotes most of its focus to Marshall's legal career, from his beginnings as a lawyer to his retirement from the U.S. Supreme Court.**

Kluger, Richard. *Simple Justice: The History of* Brown v. Board of Education *and Black America's Struggle for Equality*. New York: Knopf, 1976.

**This is the essential text for anyone wanting a thorough background of Marshall's most famous case. Kluger's book**

provides the most comprehensive coverage of *Brown v. Board* available anywhere.

Rowan, Carl T. *Dream Makers, Dream Breakers: The World of Justice Thurgood Marshall.* New York: Welcome Rain, 1993.

Written by a journalist who was also a longtime friend of Marshall's, this biography may provide the most unvarnished look at Marshall's life. Much of the material in the book comes from personal interviews conducted by the author.

*Thurgood Marshall, Associate Justice of the Supreme Court: Memorial Tributes in the Congress of the United States.* Washington, D.C.: U.S. Government Printing Office, 1994.

This collects tributes from members of Congress and from Marshall's colleagues on the Supreme Court. It also contains the complete transcript of Marshall's funeral as well as many magazine and newspaper articles that report on his death or reflect on the significance of his career.

Tushnet, Mark V. *Making Civil Rights Law: Thurgood Marshall and the Supreme Court, 1936–1961.* New York: Oxford University Press, 1994.

An excellent analysis of virtually all of Marshall's career as a lawyer, from his start in Baltimore to his appointment as an appeals court judge by President John F. Kennedy. The author is one of Marshall's former law clerks and a leading authority on Marshall and his career.

Tushnet, Mark V., ed. *Thurgood Marshall: His Speeches, Writings, Arguments, Opinions, and Reminiscences.* Chicago: Lawrence Hill, 2001.

**This is a first-rate collection of primary source materials on Marshall, including a rare, lengthy interview conducted by a scholar from the Columbia Oral History Project in 1977.**

Williams, Juan. *Thurgood Marshall: American Revolutionary.* New York: Three Rivers Press, 1998.

**Perhaps the definitive biography of Marshall, written by an established journalist who had access to Marshall and to some of his personal papers. The work is complemented by meticulous research that verifies or debunks some commonly circulated information on Marshall.**

# WEB SITES

America's Story from America's Library, "Thurgood Marshall."
www.americaslibrary.gov/cgi-bin/page.cgi/aa/marshallthrgd

Brown v. Board of Education National Historic Site.
www.nps.gov/brvb

An Interactive Civil Rights Chronology.
www.yale.edu/lawweb/jbalkin/brown/1502.html

Justice Thurgood Marshall, A Selected Bibliography. http://
www.founders.howard.edu/moorland-spingarn/MARSHALL.
HTM

The Rise and Fall of Jim Crow.
http://www.pbs.org/wnet/jimcrow/index.html

The Supreme Court Historical Society.
www.supremecourthistory.org

"Thurgood Marshall," Federal Bureau of Investigation.
http://foia.fbi.gov/foiaindex/marshall.htm

"Thurgood Marshall Before the Court," http://www.prx.org/
pieces/1236http://americanradioworks.publicradio.org/features/
marshall/

"With an Even Hand:" Brown v. Board at Fifty.
http://www.loc.gov/exhibits/brown/brown-segregation.html

# Index

Note: Page numbers in *italics* refer to photographs.

# PHOTO CREDITS

Introduction: Bettman/CORBIS

Chapter 1: Collection of the Supreme Court of the United States

Chapter 2: Department of Special Collections and University Archives, W. E. B. Du Bois Library, University of Massachusetts–Amherst

Chapter 3: Collection of the Supreme Court of the United States

Chapter 4: Collection of the Supreme Court of the United States

Chapter 5: Prints and Photographs Division, Library of Congress

Chapter 6: Scurlock Studio Records, Archives Center, National Museum of American History, Behring Center, Smithsonian Institution

Chapter 7: Prints and Photographs Division, Library of Congress

Chapter 8: AP/Wide World Photos

Chapter 9: Prints and Photographs Division, Library of Congress

Chapter 10: Prints and Photographs Division, Library of Congress

Chapter 11: Bettman/CORBIS

Chapter 12: Bettman/CORBIS

Chapter 13: AP/Wide World Photos/Bob Daughtery

Chapter 14: Prints and Photographs Division, Library of Congress

# ACKNOWLEDGMENTS

It takes a village to produce a book, and I'm grateful to many kind villagers who helped me take this project from start to finish. For their editorial work, I owe a debt of thanks to Jill Davis for signing me up and to Tracy Gates at Viking for guiding me through to the end. The thorough attention of copy editors Janet Pascal and Kathryn Hinds helped me avoid many potentially embarrassing errors, and Jim Hoover offered helpful advice regarding photograph acquisition. For their assistance in securing photographs, I'm indebted to many people, including the staff at the Library of Congress; Kay Peterson of the Smithsonian Archives Center; Robert S. Cox at the W. E. B. Du Bois Library, University of Massachusetts; Jennifer Carpenter of the Photograph Collections, Supreme Court of the United States; Joan Carroll at AP/Wide World Photos; and Norman Curie at Corbis. Thanks to Dr. Linda R. Beito of Stillman College in Tuscaloosa, Alabama, for giving the final manuscript a careful read to check the details of African American history. The talented, efficient, and incomparable staff in the Interlibrary Loan Office at Brigham Young University made research a pleasure, and the Department of English at BYU provided generous support and encouragement for my work on this book. Special thanks to my agent, Patty Campbell, for her encouragement and friendship. Finally, I must acknowledge my wife, Elizabeth, my first and best reader, and the most wonderful friend and companion anyone could ever ask for.